Date Due

Where the Heck is

BALAHECK?

Unusual place-names from Eastern Ontario

by Michael Dawber

GSPH

Published by

GENERAL STORE
PUBLISHING HOUSE

1 Main Street, Burnstown, Ontario, Canada K0J 1G0
Telephone 1-800-465-6072 Fax (613) 432-7184

ISBN 1-896182-16-X
Printed and bound in Canada

Layout and Design by Leanne Enright
Cover Design by Tammy L. Anderson

General Store Publishing House gratefully acknowledges the assistance of the Ontario Arts Council and Canada Council.

Canadian Cataloguing in Publication Data

Dawber, Michael
 Where the heck is Balaheck?: unusual place-names from Eastern Ontario

Includes index.
ISBN 1-896182-16-X

FC3056.D38 1995   917.13'6'0014   C95-900140-9
F1056.4.D38 1995

First Printing May 1995

Where the Heck Is Balaheck?

1. Glengarry County

Apple Hill ◆ Baltic Corners ◆ Cashion's Glen ◆ Drowned Baptist Creek◆ Dunvegan
Fassifern ◆ Gleneirre ◆ Glen Falloch ◆ Glen Walter ◆ Kenyon◆ Lochiel ◆ Lochinvar
Notfield ◆ Rigaud River ◆ Skye ◆ St. Elmo ◆ South La Graisse ◆ Tyotown

2. Stormont County

Black River ◆ Cahore ◆ Cannamore ◆ Ingleside ◆ Lodi ◆ Mille Roches ◆ Monkland
Moulinette ◆ Osnabruck ◆ Raisin River ◆ Santa Cruz ◆ Sheik's Island
Strathglass ◆ Warina

3. Dundas County

Dundela ◆ Elma ◆ Forward ◆ Haddo ◆ Harmony ◆ Hoasic ◆ Inkerman ◆ Mountain
Pepperville ◆ Rowena ◆ Suffel ◆ Toye's Hill ◆ Vinegar Hill

4. Prescott County

Baie des Atocas ◆ Blue Corner ◆ Caledonia Flats ◆ Carratraca Springs
Chard ◆ Chute à Blondeau ◆ Curran ◆ Fenaghvale ◆ George's Lake
La Renouche ◆ L'Orignal ◆ Le Foulon ◆ Longueuil ◆ The Pitch-Off ◆ Ritchance
Rockdale Tower ◆ The Rollway ◆ St. Eugene ◆ St. Isidore de Prescott ◆ Val Nation

5. Russell County

Borromée ◆ Embrun ◆ Girvan ◆ Hurtubise ◆ Limoges ◆ Lithia Station ◆ Navan
Orient ◆ Pana Station ◆ St-Albert ◆ St-Paschal-Baylon ◆ Sarsfield ◆ South Nation River

6. Carleton County (Region Of Ottawa-Carleton)

Ballinvilla ◆ Carp ◆ Cathartic ◆ Clandeboye ◆ Corkery ◆ Dunrobin
Hazeldean ◆ Jockvale ◆ Kars ◆ Malakoff ◆ March ◆ Mechanicsville
The Mer Bleue ◆ Naev Meehal ◆ Torbolton ◆ Vars ◆ Windfall ◆ Woodlawn

7. Grenville County

Blue Church Road ◆ Farmers Union ◆ Garryowen ◆ Glen Smail ◆ Gower (South)
The Island ◆ Jasper ◆ Kilmarnock ◆ Mild View ◆ Wolford Chapel ◆ Yule

8. Leeds County

Anoma Lea ◆ Ballycanoe ◆ Bastard ◆ Chaffeys Locks ◆ The Devil's Door Road
Fiddler's Elbow ◆ Forfar ◆ Furnace Falls ◆ Glen Elbe ◆ Ivy Lea ◆ Jellyby
Kalaria Island ◆ Lake Eloida ◆ The Lake Fleet Islands ◆ Lyn ◆ Lyndhurst
Mudlunta Island ◆ Nauvoo (Elgin) ◆ Plum Hollow ◆ Poonamalie
Locks ◆ Redan ◆ Tincap ◆ Toniata ◆ Ynyscrag Island

9. Lanark County

Arklan ◆ Clyde Forks ◆ The Cuckoo's Nest ◆ The Derry ◆ Elphin ◆ Flower Station
Folger Station ◆ Granny Cumming's Corner ◆ Lammermoor
Lavant ◆ Lodore ◆ Micaville ◆ Mopeville ◆ Numogate ◆ Ochil
Poland ◆ Rosetta ◆ Uneeda ◆ Wemyss ◆ Wilbur Station

10. Renfrew County

Ashdad ◆ Balmer's Island ◆ Bissett Creek ◆ Black Donald Lake ◆ Bullies Acre
Chenaux ◆ Cormac ◆ Dacre ◆ Deux-Rivières ◆ Eeyore Lake ◆ Foymount
Jeffreys Lake ◆ Kaszuby ◆ Khartum ◆ La Passe ◆ Moor Lake Station
The Newfoundout ◆ Osceola ◆ Paugh Lake ◆ Quadeville ◆ Rocher Fendu
Schutt ◆ Shady Nook ◆ Simpson's Pit ◆ Stonecliffe ◆ Tatty Hill ◆ Waba
Wilno ◆ Woermke ◆ Woito ◆ Wolfe Rapids ◆ Zadow

11. Frontenac County

Arden ◆ Ardoch ◆ Ballynahinch ◆ Bellrock ◆ Bellybutton Centre ◆ Brewers Mills
Buckshot ◆ Buzztown ◆ Canonto ◆ Cataraqui ◆ Crotch Lake ◆ Deerdoch
Fermoy ◆ Fernleigh ◆ Harlowe ◆ Harrowsmith ◆ Herchmer's Nose ◆ Kennebec
Lake Opinicon ◆ Lantana ◆ Mississagagon Lake ◆ Mosque Lake ◆ Myers Cave
Oconto ◆ Ompah ◆ Ore Chimney ◆ Oso ◆ Ossa ◆ Plevna ◆ Seouls Corners
Sharbot Lake ◆ Snow Road Station ◆ Spike's Corners ◆ The Star of the East
Tichborune ◆ Ungava ◆ Zanesville

12. Lennox & Addington County

Abinger ◆ Balaheck ◆ Balentra ◆ Cawdor ◆ Cloyne ◆ Comer's Mills ◆ Denbigh
Enterprise ◆ Festubert ◆ Gretna ◆ Kaladar ◆ Lens Station ◆ Massanoga
Mazinaw Lake ◆ Millhaven ◆ Posthaven ◆ Rob Roy ◆ Rogues' Hollow
The Rough Cast School ◆ Skootamatta River ◆ Stella ◆ Vennachar
Violet ◆ Weslemkoon ◆ Westplain ◆ Woodmucket ◆ Yarker

13. Prince Edward County

Bald Head ◆ Cape Vesey ◆ Carrying Place ◆ Consecon ◆ Cressy ◆ Demorestville
False Ducks Island ◆ Glenora ◆ Huyck's Point ◆ Muscote Bay ◆ Point Petre
Point Traverse ◆ Quinte ◆ Rossmore ◆ Scoharie Road ◆ Scotch Bonnet ◆ Sheba's
Island ◆ Soup Harbor ◆ Waupoos ◆ Wicked Point ◆ Woodrous ◆ Yerexville

14. Hastings County

Actinolite ◆ Astra ◆ Batawa ◆ Bird's Creek ◆ Bonarlaw ◆ Corbyville ◆ Deloro
Eldorado ◆ Elzevir ◆ Fort Stewart ◆ Foxboro ◆ Hartsmere ◆ Havergal ◆ Hermon
Hybla ◆ Ivanhoe ◆ Kamaniskeg Lake ◆ L'Amable ◆ Lost Channel ◆ Maynooth
Moira ◆ Musclow ◆ Oxenden ◆ Paudash ◆ St. Ola ◆ Shannonville ◆ Sine ◆ Stoco
Sulphide ◆ Tara ◆ Thanet ◆ Tuftsville ◆ Umfraville ◆ Upper Hermon

15. Northumberland County

Baltimore ◆ The Breakaway ◆ Camborne ◆ Cankerville ◆ Cat Hollow ◆ Cramahe
Ganaraska River ◆ Godolphin ◆ Gosport ◆ Hoard's Station ◆ Loughbreeze ◆ Menie
Mina ◆ Ongley ◆ Orland ◆ Penryn ◆ Percy Boom ◆ Red Cloud ◆ Shelter Valley
Shiloh ◆ Skibbereen ◆ Stoney Lonesome ◆ Twelve O'Clock Point ◆ Wooler

16. Peterborough County

Apsley ◆ Asphodel ◆ Boschink ◆ Buckhorn ◆ Catchacoma ◆ Chandos ◆ Chemong
Clanricarde ◆ Clarina ◆ Cottesloe ◆ Douro ◆ Dummer ◆ Kasshabog Lake
Lasswade ◆ Misquaa Ziibi ◆ Nephton ◆ Nogies Creek ◆ Serpent Mounds
Viamede ◆ Warsaw

17. Haliburton County

Allsaw ◆ Aunt Sarah's Lookout ◆ Bicroft ◆ Boskung ◆ Devil's Creek
Elephant Lake ◆ Eyre ◆ Furnace Falls ◆ Gelert ◆ Gooderham ◆ Hotspur
Irondale ◆ Ironsides ◆ Kennisis Lake ◆ Kilcoo Camp ◆ Lake Kashagawigamog
Lochlin ◆ Oxtongue Lake ◆ Paudash Lake ◆ Rackety ◆ Radium Springs
Tory Hill ◆ Ursa ◆ Wilberforce

18. The Old County of Durham

Antioch ◆ Cadmus ◆ Caesarea ◆ Cairo ◆ Cavan ◆ Charlecote ◆ Courtice
Dranoel Station ◆ Guide Board ◆ Kelmar ◆ Lotus ◆ Lovekin ◆ Osaca ◆ Peniel
Podonk Corners ◆ Pontypool ◆ Pork Hill ◆ Purple Hill ◆ Quays ◆ Scugog ◆ Solina
Stony Batter ◆ Welcome ◆ Yelverton

19. Victoria County

Aros ◆ Baddow ◆ Bobcaygeon ◆ Bolsover ◆ Burnt River ◆ The City of Peace
Coboconk ◆ Dongola ◆ Feir's Mill ◆ Fingerboard ◆ Glenarm ◆ Hardscrabble
Hell's Half Acre ◆ Islay ◆ Kinmount ◆ Little Britain ◆ Manilla ◆ Mount Horeb
Ops ◆ Rohallion ◆ Sadowa ◆ Upnor ◆ Valentia ◆ Verulam

20. Nipissing District: The Upper Madawaska

Airy ◆ Aylen Lake ◆ Lyell ◆ Opeongo ◆ Sabine

Introduction

Where the Heck is Balaheck? is not intended to be a comprehensive look at the place names of Eastern Ontario. Several authors have already made a good stab at recording all the major place-name origins. For example, Nick and Helma Mika have discussed most of the origins of the incorporated townships, villages, towns, and cities of Ontario in their *Places of Ontario* (3 volumes, 1977-1983). A great source on the township names is Herbert Gardiner's *Nothing But Names* (1899), a mammoth research effort that should be required reading for anyone interested in the place names of our province. Floreen Carter's *Ghost and Post Offices of Ontario* (1986) isn't intended to be a book on place-name origins, but her diligent work has turned up origins for many smaller villages in Ontario. Alan Rayburn, a noted place names expert, also has a book forthcoming on the place-names of Ontario.

With most of this material already available, I wanted to do something different. I tried to track down the origins of the strange, unusual names, the names of tiny hamlets that never make it into major place name studies. I was particularly interested in names that aren't on the map—like the Breakaway in Northumberland County, or Frontenac County's classic Bellybutton Centre!—because these names are in danger of being lost. The oldest generation today are almost the last people to have seen the pioneer period of Eastern Ontario firsthand. When they're gone, a huge piece of our history will be gone, too, unless we work to preserve it now.

I tried to stick to a few rules in picking place-names for *Where the Heck is Balaheck?* Generally, I've excluded the following: township names, unless they're really unusual, like Canonto or Asphodel; the names of incorporated towns and villages; and places obviously named for the first settler or postmaster, unless the name is atypical or has a story behind it. However, any community with a good story to tell, even if the story is fairly well known (like that of Apple Hill), can probably be found in here. Occasionally I've bent the rules to throw in a few personal favorites of mine, and if I rattle on I hope you'll bear with me. A couple of really contentious place names, like Gananoque and Barrys Bay, have been set aside—the debates about their origins have gone on for years, and there are many sources you can consult about them.

Each of the counties in Eastern Ontario has its own chapter because every county has unique characteristics that have shaped its place-names. The Famine Irish left their mark on Dundas, Grenville, Leeds, Carleton, and Peterborough. The Scots were the dominant group in Glengarry, and to a great extent still are in Lanark. The Loyalists used mostly British names along the St. Lawrence and the north shore of Lake Ontario. Hundreds of aboriginal names celebrate the presence of many First Nations in Eastern Ontario. The Germans in Renfrew, the Cornish in central Northumberland, the scattered pockets of Quakers . . . their migration to the counties of Eastern Ontario can be traced in the distribution of place names we have today.

I want to thank the people who helped make this book happen: the staff of Ontario's Geographic Names Board and the federal Canadian Permanent Committee on Geographical Names; the Oso Township Historical Society; Prof. Bruce Elliott; Bill McCormick; Ian Bowering and the SD&G Historical Society; Alan Rayburn of Canadian Geographic for his encouragement; Cliff Couch of Apsley; the many postmasters—especially D. M. Agnew (Wilberforce), S. Brisson (Limoges), Pauline D'Aoust (Chute à Blondeau), Lois Munro (Deux-Rivières), Jane Rolfe (Kinmount), and Sgt. Mike Valley (Astra)—who answered my inquiries; Bill Watt and the Pioneer Club of Cloyne; the staff of the Hastings Museum; Elizabeth Mitchell at the Hastings County Historical Society; Mark McMillan; General Store Publishing, for giving me the chance to indulge my long-standing interest in place-names; and the hundreds of people around Eastern Ontario who took the time to share their stories with me.

Michael Dawber
Snow Road Station, ON

I. Glengarry County

Glengarry—a small, irregular rectangle wedged against the Québec border—is the easternmost county in Ontario. As its name suggests, Glengarry was settled almost entirely by Scots, and Scottish names cover the landscape here. Only later did francophones from neighboring Prescott move into Glengarry's northern concessions—today, almost half the population of this one-time Scottish stronghold are of French descent. The Glengarry name remains, remembering the deep valley of Loch Garry in Scotland's Highlands Region. In Scottish Gaelic (a language once heard as often as English in Glengarry County), the name "Glengarry" means "valley of the rushing water." Glengarry counts among its leading citizens the first premier of Ontario, Sandfield Macdonald, who was born in Charlottenburg Township.

◆◆ ❖ ◆◆

APPLE HILL. The village of Apple Hill has a well-loved story behind its name. When the Canadian Pacific Railway was built through town, the tracks were laid directly over an apple orchard. The orchard was owned by an influential local Conservative, Sandy Kennedy. Around the same time, the federal government (which was also Conservative) decided to grant a post office to the village. When the office opened in 1882, it did so under a name suggested by Kennedy to recall his lost orchard: Apple Hill. Apple Hill P.O. still operates in Kenyon Township.

BALTIC CORNERS. This little village has had its name misspelled so often it's hard to know what the name was intended to be. In 1881, the government granted a post office to a Lancaster Township farming family—either at their suggestion or at the government's discretion, the office was named "Baltic P. O." Within a few months, the office shut down. Then, in 1884, another office was granted at this same location, apparently under the name "Baltic's Corners." However, through a copying error or some bad handwriting, the name was read as "Baltie's Corners," and so entered in the official records. Around the same time, someone else misread the name as "Battie's Corners," and this name was also added to the records. The office was shut down in 1889, but the mix-up in the records was never cleared up, leaving the impression there were two different offices here. The official name is now "Baltic Corners."

CASHION'S GLEN. This is an attractive old post office name from Charlottenburg Township. The name was given by Mrs. Caroline Cashion, a Scottish farmer who became the hamlet's first postmistress in 1874. On some maps the name is misspelled as "Cushion's Glen."

DROWNED BAPTIST CREEK. This arresting name was locally applied to the Delisle River. As told by Ewan Ross, the community of Dominionville on the Delisle once had a Baptist congregation. As was traditional in their church, the Baptists practised baptism, using the Delisle for this purpose. One Sunday, the minister was baptizing some new adherents when he accidentally lost one elderly convert in the flowing river. The minister looked up and said to another church-goer, "Brother, the Lord giveth and the Lord taketh away. Pass me another."

DUNVEGAN. The Kenyon Township community of Dunvegan might have been inspired to choose its name by nearby Skye P.O. (see below). The original Dunvegan, a Scottish castle, overlooks a deep fjord on the Isle of Skye's west coast. The name "Dunvegan" has been used across Canada, appearing as a place-name in Nova Scotia, Ontario (our Kenyon Township village), Alberta, and the Northwest Territories. In each case, the word was probably carried abroad by members of the Clan Macleod, whose ancestral seat is Dunvegan Castle. The castle is said to have inspired its own name—in ancient Brythonic, the language from which modern Gaelic is descended, Dunvegan means "little castle." In an apparent contradiction, though, Dunvegan is a huge castle.

FASSIFERN. Fassifern hamlet is another unmistakably Scottish name in Lochiel Township. Originally, the community's post office was to have been called Kennedy, after an elderly resident of the area. However, other Lochiel residents objected to this proposal, made by a government official in Ottawa. A stream of other names flooded in, and eventually the government decided on "Fassifern"—Lord Fassifern was a prominent Scottish noble. As Lord Fassifern was from the Clan Cameron, the suggestion of his name was warmly received by his many clansmen in Lochiel Township. The post office which sparked this pitched battle closed in 1915.

GLENEIRRE. The community now called Glendale in Charlottenburg was once known unofficially as "Gleneirre." Like Naev Meehal (see Carleton), Gleneirre is a phonetic spelling of a Gaelic name—the Gaelic-speaking Scots knew the village as *GleannFheoir*, "Hay's Glen." Sgt. John Hay was one of the first settlers in the area, and his descendants were prominent citizens in Charlottenburg. The dull name Glendale came from a nearby cheese factory.

GLEN FALLOCH. Glen Falloch (pronounced "FAHL-uck") in Charlottenburg remembers a Scottish valley, now part of Scotland's Central Region. The River Falloch runs south-west through the valley towards Loch Lomond. Glen Falloch hamlet in Canada never grew large enough for a post office, and remains a quiet crossroads on SDG County Road 20. In Gaelic, *falloch* means "hidden," and the description fits the secluded location of Glen Falloch.

GLEN WALTER. One of the larger villages in Glengarry, Glen Walter is located near Cornwall in Charlottenburgh Township. The traditional story behind the name is that there were a number of men named "Walter" living in or near the village. For this reason, the postmaster (who *wasn't* named Walter, incidentally) decided on the name "Glen Walter" in 1874. If there's a Glen Walter in Scotland—the most likely source for any name in Glengarry—then it's well hidden.

KENYON. The distinctive name of Kenyon Township remembers an English politician, Lloyd, Lord Kenyon. From 1782 'til 1788, Lord Kenyon was the attorney-general of England, and he later became a judge. His name was first applied to this township, in Glengarry's northwestern corner, around 1798. Kenyon took his title from a British community, now surrounded by the industrial city of Manchester. In Old Welsh, Kenyon might have meant "the hill (or mound) of a man called Einion."

LOCHIEL. Lochiel Township is in the northeastern part of Glengarry. It was the last township added to Glengarry, split off from neighboring Lancaster around 1820. The beautiful name Lochiel (pronounced lock-EEL) is, naturally, Scottish: Lochiel was the estate of the chiefs of the Clan Cameron, a Highland clan well represented among Glengarry's early settlers. The name came from a small lake, now called Loch Eil by the Scottish. The great castle of Lochiel was destroyed by fire in 1746, burned by an invading English army during a Scottish uprising. An old poem warns the Clan Cameron of such danger from the South: "Lochiel, Lochiel, beware the day," it says, "when the Lowland shall meet in battle array."

LOCHINVAR. Little Lochinvar is a hamlet on the Rigaud River, near the Lochiel-West Hawkesbury border. Between 1871 and 1890, three different post offices here were all called Lochinvar, and the name persisted long after the office closed. The name Lochinvar is familiar to readers of Sir Walter Scott—the hero of his novel *Marmion* was Young Lochinvar, who took his title from a fortress in a small Scottish loch. In Gaelic, the phrase *loch an bharra* means "the lake on the height," the original Lochinvar being in the rugged hills of Dumfries & Galloway.

NOTFIELD. This long-abandoned name from Kenyon Township has a confusing and murky history. When the river-front townships were first created, the government intended to leave a strip of land between Stormont and Glengarry Counties as a First Nations reserve. Some early maps of the area clearly show parts of Charlottenburg and Kenyon Townships as "Indian Land." In 1809, the name of this reserve was recorded as Nutfield, probably after Nutfield town in Surrey, England. This planned reserve was never established, but it's possible the name "Nutfield" lingered on and was remembered as Notfield. Some sixty years later, when a post office opened near the intended reserve lands, the first postmaster called it Notfield. Local histories place Notfield P.O. near Dominionville, and in 1874 customers of Notfield were switched to Dominionville. The mysterious name hasn't been in regular use since then.

RIGAUD RIVER. This name is a new addition to the landscape in Glengarry. The river was originally known as the La Graisse (see South La Graisse, below), but to conform to its French name downstream in Québec, "La Graisse" was replaced by "Rigaud." The name has strong historic links to Glengarry. In the 1730s, Philippe de Rigaud, Marquis of Vaudreuil, owned two seigneuries here at what was then the edge of organized French settlement. (Both his family name and his title are still in use as place-names in Québec.) This river crossed both his properties before entering the St. Lawrence near the Island of Montréal.

SKYE. Skye Post Office once operated on the Kenyon-Caledonia line, just north of modern Highway 417. The Isle of Skye is part of Scotland's extensive Western Isles, the rocky, wind-swept home of many Glengarry settlers (possibly including J. McKenzie, the Ontario Skye's first postmaster). The name "Skye" comes from the Gaelic word *sgaith*, meaning "wing." From the Scottish mainland, Skye seems to sweep upwards into two wings of hills from a central plain. The spelling of the name has been influenced by the English word "sky."

ST. ELMO. There are hundreds of communities in Canada named for Christian saints, including a bewildering array of St. Johns, St. Thomases, and St. Marys. However, this is the only Canadian community to remember the patron saint of sailors, St. Elmo. Elmo, who died around a.d. 300, was revered by sailors on the Mediterranean Sea. A glow around ship masts, caused by electrical discharges during thunderstorms, was christened "St. Elmo's Fire" in his honor. Curiously, St. Elmo P.O. operated well inland, near Maxville in Kenyon Township. An old story says "St. Elmo" was suggested by the first postmaster's daughter—she had seen the saint's name mentioned in a novel.

SOUTH LA GRAISSE. For a few years after Confederation, there was a South La Graisse P.O. on the 3rd Line of Lochiel. The name is French—the literal translation is "oil" or "fat," but La Graisse may be a corruption of the French phrase *la grâce* (grace). The office took its name from the La Graisse River, which has since been renamed the Rigaud (see above). Local residents often called the La Graisse "the Grass River," not because of any particular feature of the land, but just from the similarity of the sounds. The La Graisse was probably named during the French regime, as many French names from the pre-Conquest years were later picked up by the Scots.

TYOTOWN. The strange name of Tyotown, a village in southern Charlottenburg Township, comes from the hamlet's first postmaster. In 1887, Joseph H. Tyo applied for and received a post office. Like many other newly minted postmasters, Tyo decided to name his office for himself.

2. Stormont County

By population, Stormont is the largest partner of the United Counties of Stormont, Dundas, & Glengarry (usually shortened to "SD&G"). Stormont contains the county seat of Cornwall, and the so-called "Lost Villages," seven communities that were flooded when the St. Lawrence Seaway was created. Their history, and their names, are still celebrated in the area. In the early days of settlement, Stormont's population was more diverse than that of Dundas or of Glengarry, including Germans (who settled in Osnabruck Township), Irish, and Scots. The county itself bears a Scottish name—David Murray, Viscount Stormont, was a major political figure in 18th century Scotland. However, "Stormont" also has a 20th century connection in Ireland—the short-lived Northern Irish parliament titled itself Stormont.

BLACK RIVER. See Raisin River.

CAHORE. Little Cahore, in northwestern Finch Township, was briefly the site of a rural post office. The name strikes one as possibly East Indian (it sounds like the city of Lahore in Pakistan), but "Cahore" is actually in Ireland. A small promontory on the east coast of Wexford, about equidistant from the cities of Wicklow and Wexford, is known as Cahore Point. It's not a coincidence the name Ballycanew, from a town by Ireland's Cahore, also appears near our own Cahore (see Ballycanoe under Leeds County). Many Wexford Irish immigrated to Ontario, so we should expect to find at least a few Wexford place names in our neck of the woods.

CANNAMORE. Cannamore was right down the road from Cahore P.O., only a few kilometres away from the town of Forget in Russell County. A post office operated in Cannamore for sixty years, up until the first months of World War II. The word *cannamore* is almost certainly Scottish—there are at least three places in the Highlands bearing the name (spelled Ceanna Mòr or Ceannamor), which means simply "big hill." Scottish King Malcolm III, who reigned from 1058 until 1093, was also nicknamed "Canmore" because of his large head.

An alternative explanation comes from local tradition that says the name came from an off-hand remark. At a public meeting to name the village's new post office, one Scottish villager pressed for a choice threw up his hands and said, "I canna no more think of a name."Someone picked up on his response and suggested "Cannamore." A little far-fetched, maybe!

INGLESIDE. Ingleside was created in the 1950s to accept people dislocated by the St. Lawrence Seaway project. There was a long, fierce argument over what this community should be called. Many proposals—including Avondale, Sunnydale, Kanata, and Wales (the name of one of the Lost Villages)—were batted around until residents finally accepted "Ingleside." The name Ingleside was suggested by someone who had seen a house so called in nearby Aultsville. The accepted origin of Ingleside is Scottish Gaelic, in which "Ingleside" means "the side of the hearth." However, it's also possible the home took its name from the Welsh town called Ingleside, found in South Glamorgan County.

LODI & STRATHGLASS. The Roxborough Township hamlet of Lodi, near Moose Creek, seems to draw its name from continental Europe. Lodi is a community in Italy's Lombardy Province, southeast of Milan. Italian names are extremely rare in Ontario, so how this one came to be in Roxborough is a mystery. The Lodi Post Office was known as Strathglass and Roxborough West during the 1850s and 1860s, but Lodi is the only name that has survived. It's possible the name arrived here via the United States, as there are several "Lodis" in the U.S. with which local residents might have been familiar.

As for Strathglass, the name comes from a river valley in Scotland's Inver-nesshire (now Highlands Region). "Strath" is the anglicized version of the Gaelic srath, "valley," and the River Glass takes its name from an ancient Celtic word for "stream."

MILLES ROCHES. See Moulinette.

MONKLAND. The town of Monkland has had its current name only since 1966, when "Monckland Station" became simply "Monkland." Monckland Station was itself not the community's first name. In 1854, the village was originally called "Roxborough Post Office," from its location in Roxborough Township. In 1862, the name "Monckland" was substituted—it's believed the name was taken from the governor-general's then-official residence of Monklands in Montréal. The "ck" spelling was used to honor the governor at the time, Charles Stanley Monck, who became Canada's first post-Confedera-tion G-G. The unusual spelling of his surname influenced several Ontario place names, including the Monck Settlement Road and a provincial riding in the Niagara area. The original Monkland, in England's Hereford & Worcester

County, was known as the home of a monastic sect—thus, literally, "Monkland." When our Monckland received a Canadian Pacific station in the 1880s, the community was renamed Monckland Station to reflect this new role. After passenger rail service ended, the "Station" was dropped, along with the "ck."

MOULINETTE & MILLE ROCHES. Moulinette is one of the "Lost Villages," a half-dozen communities that disappeared under the St. Lawrence Seaway. Moulinette used to stand on the river shore about eleven kilometres west of Cornwall—a small island in the St. Lawrence, close to the former town site, is now called Moulinette Is. The name means "small mill" in French, and in the early 1800s a grist mill was built there by one John Dixon.

The history of the name "Moulinette" is somewhat confusing. Moulinette Post Office was first established in the neighboring community of Mille Roches (meaning "thousand rocks," a description of nearby rapids in the St. Lawrence). For about thirty years, there were two Moulinettes on the map: the post office and the original town. In 1859, Moulinette P. O. became Mille Roches P. O. , ending the confusion. It wasn't until 1874 that the Moulinette got its own post office under its own name . . . only to lose it again when the seaway flooded town.

OSNABRUCK. Osnabruck Township, in southwestern Stormont, remembers Calvinist Germans who came to Eastern Ontario during the Loyalist migration. The government recognized their presence with this name, which stands out among the largely English names of the other shoreline townships. The original Osnabrück is a city in northwestern Germany, part of the modern province of Lower Saxony. The name was probably chosen because Osnabrück was in the Kingdom of Hanover—the reigning British monarch during the Loyalist settlement, George III, was part of Hanover's royal family. Osnabruck has also been written as Osnaburgh and as "Oznaburg," which was apparently the name of an early Stormont post office.

RAISIN RIVER & BLACK RIVER. The Raisin is one of the largest rivers in Eastern Ontario, and like the South La Graisse (see Glengarry County), the Raisin's name dates back to New France. "Raisin" is the French word for "grape," and wild grapes can still be found in the Raisin's watershed. The source of the name is more obvious in the river's original title, "Rivière aux Raisins" (river of the grapes). The upper part of the river was also known as the Black, chiefly because of the river's source. The Raisin rises near the Newington Bog, and the water leaving the Bog is extremely silty—thus, the "black" river. This nickname was used only above St. Andrew's West, while below, the river was always called the Raisin. A railway station near Harrisons Corners was known as Black River Station from the nickname. A post office in Lancaster Township, Glengarry County, was also called "Rivière Raisin" from 1865 to 1880.

SANTA CRUZ. Santa Cruz hamlet used to stand between Moulinette and Woodlands, two of the Lost Villages on the St. Lawrence. The name simply means "saint (or sainted) cross" and comes from Portugal where the heavily Catholic population has named dozens of towns Santa Cruz. It's not clear how this Santa Cruz ended up in Osnabruck Township. A popular local explanation says, during the days of New France, a group of Portuguese sailors somehow got lost, ended up down the St. Lawrence, and landed here. They stayed long enough to erect a cross and call the spot "Santa Cruz" before sailing on. There's no evidence this ever happened, but it makes a great story!

SHEIK'S ISLAND. This name conjures up images of a mysterious Middle Eastern visitor to the Cornwall area. However, the spelling of "Sheik's"—an island partially submerged by the St. Lawrence Seaway Project—is misleading. David Sheek settled on this island in 1806, having leased it from the St. Regis Mohawks. His name was later given to the island, though Sheek has been misspelled in a bewildering number of ways, including "Sheik."

STRATHGLASS. See Lodi.

WARINA. Only part of the story behind Warina's name has been passed down to us. The village, which is on Highway 138 in Roxborough Township, was named by postmaster A. Munro for a place he found in a novel. Unfortunately, the name of the novel isn't included in the story. There might be some connection to Warin, a town in Germany, given the number of German settlers in Stormont. Warina Post Office closed up shop in 1913.

3. Dundas County

Dundas—named for Henry Dundas, a long-serving British cabinet minister of the 1700s—is the most heavily Irish county in the Stormont, Dundas, & Glengarry federation. Most of these Irish came during the 1840s, fleeing the Potato Famine to resettle in Canada. In many counties, their settlement can be seen in the Irish place-names they gave to their new communities. In Dundas, however, the four townships and the half-dozen or so major towns had already been named by the Loyalists. As a result, Irish names tend to be found only on the smaller villages or on post offices dating to the late 1800s. This is particularly the case in Winchester Township: while the larger villages (Winchester and Chesterville) have English names, among the smaller hamlets are Connaught, Limerick, and The Boyne, all distinctively Irish.

DUNDELA. This small crossroads village (known as MacIntosh's Corners in the early days) stands on SDG Road 18 in Matilda Township. The village is famous as home of the MacIntosh Apple—started from a single tree, the MacIntosh has now become the most popular apple in North America. While the name Dundela has a decided Irish ring to it, the origin has proven very elusive. One story says the hamlet's post office was named for a Miss Delia Dillabough, the daughter of a successful Matilda Township farmer, James Dillabough. If this is true, then the name may be a play on words, as Dundee is a well-known Irish town. However, there is a more direct link to Ireland: in Dún Laoghaire, a city near Dublin, there is a neighborhood known as Dundela Park. In either case, Dundela became a Canadian place-name when Dundela P. O. opened in 1866.

ELMA. The village of Elma is on SDG Road 7 in Matilda Township. "Elma" sounds as if it might be a female Christian name, taken from a local settler. The most likely source, though, is the town of Elma in Erie County, New York State. Our Elma was named in 1884, possibly from the post office department's list of American place-names (see "Little Britain" under Victoria County). Equally likely, the settlers of Dundas County—many of them expatriate American Loyalists—would have known the original town. The name "Elma" was inspired by a large elm which once stood in the centre of Elma, N. Y. A second possible source is Lady Elma Bruce, the daughter of Canadian governor Lord Elgin. A township in Southwestern Ontario was named "Elma" in her honor.

FORWARD. Forward hamlet is almost part of Chesterville, situated just west of Chesterville's municipal boundaries. Forward's name seems to reflect the drive for settlement and expansion that was prized among the pioneering Loyalists of Eastern Ontario. However, the hamlet was named for a local family, the Forwards, who farmed in this part of Winchester Township. School Section No. 8, established around 1897, was also called "the Forward School"—a Thomas Forward was one of S. S. No. 8's first trustees. The school section name may have been picked up as the official place-name for this location.

HADDO. The curious name Haddo was given to a village in southwestern Matilda. The name would be well known to the people of Glengarry, but might have seemed strange to the local Irish—Haddo House is a mansion in Scotland's Grampian Region. The name is partly Old English and partly Gaelic in origin, with the combined meaning "half a pasture." It's been written the name Haddo was suggested for this hamlet by Lord Dufferin, a Canadian governor-general of the 19th century. However, it seems more likely the name was proposed by one of Dufferin's successors, the Earl of Aberdeen, as Haddo House was his family's ancestral home. As well, Haddo P. O. opened in 1894, which was during Aberdeen's term in office.

HARMONY. The hamlet of Harmony is located at a sharp curve in Highway 31, just east of the Winchester Bog. Place-names including "Harmony" and "Union" are typically Upper Canadian, stressing the (largely mythical, but dearly held!) unity of Upper Canadian society in the 1800s. This Harmony takes its name from the local church, Harmony Community Church, at R. R. 1, Winchester.

HOASIC. This confounding and bizarre place-name is found in central Williamsburgh Township, just southeast of Elma (see above). There are two possible explanations: one is that the name is an aboriginal word, written variously as "Hoosac" or "Hoosick," after which several places in the northeastern U. S. are named. The meaning of the word isn't known, but there are Hoosacs or Hoosicks in Massachusetts, New Hampshire, and Vermont. The Loyalist settlers of Dundas could have been familiar with any one of these villages, though why such an obscure word should become such a popular place-name is a mystery. Our Hoasic may also have some connection to the Hosick Lumber Company, though there's no evidence Hosick ever had any land or dealings in Dundas. In either case, the village's first postmaster, J. J. Baker, was responsible for selecting "Hoasic" in 1870.

INKERMAN. Inkerman is one of many places in Canada named during the Crimean War of the 1850s. The war occurred when settlement was still expanding in Ontario, and many new villages were inspired to name themselves for Crimean battles. The original Battle of Inkerman took place on 05 November 1854, the Russian army being defeated by the combined forces of the British and the French. That same month, a hamlet in Mountain Township was deciding on a name for its new post office—Inkerman was a popular and patriotic choice. The name became official when Inkerman P. O. opened on 01 January 1855. Several other villages in Eastern Canada took up the name Inkerman, including the community now known as Curran (see Prescott County). A Senatorial division of Québec is also called Inkerman.

MOUNTAIN. The name Mountain may seem entirely inappropriate for a township of flat farmland! The Mountain of the name isn't a physical feature, but a Québec religious figure. The Right Rev. Jacob Mountain, who lived from 1749 to 1825, was the first Anglican bishop of Québec, and was instrumental in establishing the Anglican church in that province. He was appointed to his position in 1793, and the government of Upper Canada chose to recognize him by naming this township Mountain around 1798. Reverend Mountain apparently visited Dundas County in 1794.

Two communities in the township have taken the Mountain name. One is called simply Mountain, which has been the post office name since 1888. The other community is South Mountain, which has been the postal name since 1851. Between 1861 and 1913, there was a third in this series, a "North Mountain P. O.," to correspond with South Mountain.

PEPPERVILLE (SILVER CITY). Pepperville—now known locally as Silver City—is in Mountain Township, between the villages of Mountain and South Mountain. Pepperville's name doesn't come from the spice, but from the Pepper family, that settled in the western part of the township. The hamlet never received a post office, and the name Pepperville is seldom used now.

ROWENA. Local histories say the name of Rowena hamlet, in Matilda Township, was provided by the post office department in 1880. (The name was proposed in place of the local choice, "East Matilda.") There are two other significant towns called "Rowena" in the world, one in Australia, the other in the State of Texas. Either could have been known to a post office bureaucrat, or could have been placed on a list of new post office names. There is another, more interesting possibility—in Sir Walter Scott's novel *Ivanhoe*, the wife of the title character is called Lady Rowena. Ivanhoe was earlier given as a post office name in Hastings County (see Ivanhoe under Hastings), so someone may have remembered their Scott and named the Dundas community Rowena. If Rowena was a relation of the first postmaster, Thomas S. Carter, her name has gone unrecorded in the area.

SUFFEL. This was once the name of Inkerman's railway station (see above) in Mountain Township. The station, located on SDG Road 3, and the surrounding hamlet are called "Inkerman Station" today—the name "Suffel" was originally coined to honor the local Suffel family. The Suffels owned the land on which the railway station was built, and several families of Suffels still live at Inkerman Station.

TOYE'S HILL. Toye's Hill was once the site of a rural post office in Matilda Township. The "Toye" was the first postmaster, I. Toye, who opened the post office in 1882. The name is sometimes shown as "Toyes Hill," a result of the provincial government removing apostrophes from place-names in Ontario. The change was also made to nearby Toyes Creek, which is properly Toye's Creek.

VINEGAR HILL. This name of this hamlet in Mountain Township has a special meaning to the Irish people. In 1798, a major Irish rebellion against English rule began at Vinegar Hill, near Enniscorthy in County Wexford. An ancient windmill on the Hill was used as a base by the rebels, and for a time they managed to fend off the British army. Even though the rebellion eventually failed, the attempt was celebrated for years afterwards by the Irish, including the many Irish settlers of Dundas.

4. Prescott County

Prescott is an angular county running from the Québec border up the Ottawa Valley. This is one of the most francophone counties in Southern Ontario, and there is a strong French influence in the area's place names. The francophone population migrated across the Ottawa River from Québec, largely at the instigation of the Catholic Church. The church's leaders believed the French language and culture would better survive in Canada if there were "outpost" populations in other provinces. This policy led to the settlement of Prescott which, as late as the 1850s, still had large areas of undeveloped farmland, and of parts of Northern Ontario. Prescott also has links back to the French regime of the 17th and 18th centuries—the last seigneury (or estate) granted under the regime was Longueuil, which still survives as Longueuil Township. Longueuil and several other names from that time period remain in use in Prescott.

BAIE DES ATOCAS. The Baie des Atocas is part of the Ottawa River, curving into the shoreline of Longueuil Township. Many of the place-names in Longueuil come from the French era, and Baie des Atocas is no exception. The name means "the bay of cranberries," and cranberries were plentiful along the low-lying, marshy shore of Longueuil.

BLUE CORNER. This intersection on the Alfred-Longueuil townline has a great tale to its name. Back in the Second World War, there used to be a popular dance hall here. The dance hall was painted blue, and so the under-thirty crowd that partied here starting calling this "Blue Corner." The hall has since burned down, but the intersection of Highway 17 and the Caledonia Springs Road is still called Blue Corner locally.

CALEDONIA FLATS. See Fenaghvale.

CARRATRACA SPRINGS (PLANTAGENET STATION). The community of Plantagenet Station, in North Plantagenet Township, was once called Carratraca Springs. The exotic-sounding name has fallen out of use, but we can still track its origin back to Andalusia in Spain. A Spanish village called

Carratraca was a popular tourist destination in the late 1800s because of its mineral hot springs. Hot springs and spas were a Victorian-era health fad, and any spring worth its salt (so to speak) was seized as a potential money-maker. This fad also spread to Eastern Ontario, and several communities—including Carlsbad Springs (see Carleton County) and Plantagenet Station—had spa resorts.

CHARD. This Somerset village name appeared on a local post office from 1879 to 1915. The choice of Chard may have been made by the first postmaster —Bill Brown of North Plantagenet Township—as Chard is one of the few place-names in Prescott with a British origin. The original village of Chard in Somerset was named during the Dark Ages. In Old English, the word *cert* (pronounced "cherd") meant "a rough pasture or field," and the place-name Chard developed from this description.

CHUTE À BLONDEAU. One of the most attractive place names in Prescott, Chute à Blondeau (or "Blondeau's Rapids" in English) has several romantic stories explaining its origin. All of them involve a backwoodsman named Blondeau, who lived somewhere near these rapids on the Ottawa. One story makes Blondeau a long-struggling fisherman—in one lean season, desperate to feed his family, Blondeau ventured into the rapids trying to catch any fish he could. Despite his tremendous physical strength, Blondeau was unable to keep his canoe upright and was thrown into the boiling rapids. Blondeau's wife dove into the river to save him, and almost did, but the current also carried her away. Another story says Blondeau was a foolhardy voyageur who was killed trying to shoot the rapids. In his memory, the rapids became known as Chute à Blondeau.

There was a long debate in this century about whether Chute à Blondeau should be spelled with or without dashes (i.e., Chute-à-Blondeau). It is the custom in French to use dashes for a name like this, but generally the dashes have been omitted in Ontario. The Permanent Secretariat on Geographic Names eventually decided to take the dashes out, and that later became the usage for the local post office. Chute à Blondeau P.O. first opened in 1871 as "Chute <u>au</u> Blondeau" in East Hawkesbury.

CURRAN. The name of Curran village in North Plantagenet indicates either Irish settlers in this vicinity, or a proud Irish patriot in the post office department. John Philpot Curran, an Irish MP and lawyer, became a hero of the Irish independence movement when he defended the leaders of the 1798 rebellion. (See Vinegar Hill under Dundas County for more details.) In spite of this defence, he retained considerable influence with Ireland's British masters until his death in 1817. Part of the town of Larne, in County Antrim, has been named

"Curran" in his honor. North Plantagenet's Curran has had this name since 1858—previous to that, the community was called Inkerman for the famous Crimean War battle. (See Inkerman, also under Dundas County.)

FENAGHVALE & CALEDONIA FLATS. This hamlet, first called "Caledonia Flats" from its location in Caledonia Township, went by the postal name "Fenaghvale" from 1861 until 1921. This part of Caledonia saw many families of Irish settlers, and one family could trace its roots back to the town of Fenagh in Ireland. The town is an ancient religious centre in County Leitrim whose Gaelic name, *Fíonacha,* means "a wooded place (or places)." The settlers took this name and added "-vale" to describe the setting of their community. Fenaghvale hamlet—which was also known informally as Croxon's Corners in the 1800s—is now down a side-road near the Alfred Bog.

GEORGE'S LAKE. An old French trapper gave his name to this shallow bay near the Ottawa River. According to local legend, the trapper—Georges—would cross over from the Québec side of the river during the winter, and trap beaver in this bay. Since then, local residents have taken to calling this "George's Lake" in his honor. The "lake" is in Alfred Township, and is now surrounded by cottages.

LA RENOUCHE. This baffling name, from a hamlet near Chute à Blondeau, has a delightful story to tell. As told by local resident Bernard Durocher, ". . . it seems that there were tow families, the Rozons and the Renauds, who owned race horses. Every day, they would train their horses down this road (the 2nd Concession of East Hawkesbury). An Irish lady, who only knew a few words in French, would say—'Here comes the racers with their *barouche.*' Barouche was the French slang word for silkey." Over time, this Irish settler's fondness for *barouche* must have been mistranslated by other anglophone settlers as *la renouche,* which (despite its convincing appearance) isn't really a word.

L'ORIGNAL. L'Orignal is probably Prescott's most widely recognized place name, as L'Orignal town is the county seat for Prescott and Russell. The word *l'orignal,* which means "the moose" (or "the elk") in French, is properly pronounced "lor-een-YAHL." Like the surrounding Township of Longueuil (see below), L'Orignal dates back to the French regime. In 1674, one François Prévost was granted a seigneury along the Ottawa River—Prévost named this property "Pointe-à-L'Orignal," probably from the abundance of moose in the marshy land there. The name survived the Seven Years' War and was given to one of Prescott County's first post offices in 1829.

LE FOULON. From 1851 to 1862, Le Foulon Post Office was located somewhere near Chute à Blondeau in East Hawkesbury Township. As a place-name, Le Foulon has disappeared completely, but we can guess at its inspiration. In French, *le foulon* means "the Fuller," indicating there was a fulling mill nearby. It's also possible the first postmaster was himself a fuller. Before the advent of modern manufacturing, the process of "fulling" was used to prepare handmade cloth for use. At a fulling mill, the cloth was beaten, both to clean it and to force the cloth fibres to stand up. This made the cloth stronger and thicker (i.e., "fuller").

LONGUEUIL. Longueuil can claim to be the oldest township in Ontario. The current boundaries of Longueuil date back to the 17th century, when Longueuil was a French seigneury (see L'Orignal, above). The last French owner of the seigneury was Jean Le Moyne de Longueuil, from which this township and a city in Québec derive their names. The name, pronounced roughly "long-GOY," is an old-fashioned phrase meaning "the long view." Longueuil seigneury was transformed into an Ontario township around 1798, complete with the long, narrow lot system typically used by the French government. Linguist Percy Robinson wrote the Longueuil seigneury was known as Karon-hiatsikoua ("the big long sky") to the Mohawk people. It's possible Le Moyne created the name Longueuil from this Mohawk description, or that the Mohawks adapted Longueuil into their own language as Karonhiatsikoua.

THE PITCH-OFF. This name was once used for a spot above Plantagenet Station, near the South Nation River. Near the station is a low ridge, which one could "pitch off" if one lost one's footing! The name is colloquial and still known locally.

RITCHANCE. This odd name from Longueuil Township doesn't make sense until you run it back to its origin. Originally, the hamlet was called "Rue de Chance," after a road along the Ottawa River here. Translated from French, "Rue de Chance" means "chancy (i.e., hazardous or tricky) road," a meaning expressed well on another (obviously equally-perilous!) stretch of the road called "Hazard Street." Over time, Rue de Chance has become more and more clipped through local pronunciation, the "rue de" being worn down to "rit-." On some maps, the name is even more reduced as "Richance." There was a post office here, using the "Ritchance" spelling of the name, from 1905 until 1913.

ROCKDALE TOWER. One of the last post offices opened in Prescott was Rockdale Tower, located at the Brown family homestead in North Plantagenet. The name sounds as if it belongs to a castle in the Scottish highlands, but "Rockdale Tower" has its origins in Prescott. Adjacent to the Browns, a homestead owned by the Anderson family was known as Rockdale Farm, possibly from the rocky soil there. Sometime during the early 1900s, the provincial government built an observation tower—a forest fire look-out, maybe —on the Anderson property . . . thus, Rockdale Tower. The post office was at the Brown farm from 1908 to 1912.

THE ROLLWAY. The Rollway, a hamlet in North Plantagenet Township, evokes images of a rough chute or logs in the slide. As Rollway native Bill McCormick recalls, the name does come from lumbering days. "Day after day," he wrote, "teams of pounding Clydesdales and snorting black Percherons . . . would pull up alongside the high embankment of the Nation River beyond our home, under the guiding reins of a highly perched driver. The logs were then rolled down onto the river's icy surface to be floated down to Anderson's sawmill when spring would melt away the . . . ice. This is why the place became known as the Rollway." From 1908 until 1912, a post office called "The Rollway" was run by local resident Jean-Baptiste Moderie. The name is occasionally shown as just "Rollway."

ST. EUGENE. This village has been called St. Eugene since 1861, when St. Eugene P. O. opened in East Hawkesbury Township. There are many saints named Eugene—the one honored here is probably St. Eugene of Toledo, an archbishop of that Italian city who died in 657. St. Eugene is said to have been a frail, but zealous, religious leader.

ST. ISIDORE DE PRESCOTT. This incorporated village has officially dropped the "de Prescott" from its attractive name, and the post office has now followed suit. The community honors the Spaniard St. Isidore (560-636) who served as the Archbishop of Seville. St. Isidore was a prolific author and a widely respected Catholic educator in Christian Spain. Originally the village went by the Irish name "Kerry," until St. Isidore de Prescott was approved in 1882. (It was already the name of the local Catholic parish.) In French, the name is usually written with hyphens, i.e., "St-Isidore-de-Prescott." The "de Prescott" may have been added to differentiate the village from four other "St. Isidores" in Canada.

VAL NATION. See South Nation River under Russell County.

5. Russell County

Russell is now the smallest county in Ontario, having lost one of its four townships (Cumberland) to the Region of Ottawa-Carleton. (In this book, all names are given in their pre-regionalization counties, so you'll find all the Cumberland names listed here instead of under Carleton.) The remaining, L-shaped county is heavily francophone, settled by the same church-sponsored migration program that populated Prescott. Not surprisingly, given the historic connection between the two, Russell and Prescott are now linked for municipal government purposes. Irish farmers also crossed over from neighboring Carleton, adding an Irish component to the local place names. The "Russell" of the county is Peter Russell, a British ex-patriot who came to Canada with Governor John Graves Simcoe (see Wolford Chapel under Grenville County). Russell served as inspector-general in the Executive Council, which was the cabinet of its day. After Simcoe's departure, Russell was the acting governor of Upper Canada in 1797.

BORROMÉE. This old post office name can still be found on the 10th Line of Cumberland Township, though Borromée has been incorrectly spelled as "Burromee" on several maps. Following the pattern of many francophone communities in Eastern Ontario, the hamlet is named for a saint, St-Charles-Borromée. Known as St. Carlo Borromeo in his native Italy, the saint died in 1584 aged only forty-six. He was the Archbishop of Milan and was remembered as having helped thousands of peasants survive a plague in 1578. Our Borromée Post Office opened in 1885 and closed exactly thirty years later in 1915.

EMBRUN. The town of Embrun, in Russell Township, has had its current name since the post office opened in November, 1858. The name Embrun (not "Embru_m_," as it's occasionally shown) was suggested by the vicar at nearby Sarsfield—the vicar had done some of his theological studies at Embrun, France. A conflicting version of the story says francophone homesteaders originally called the town "St. Jacques d'Embrun," in echo of their home parish in Québec, St. Jacques-de-l'Achigan. When the post office was granted, the government shortened the name to just "Embrun." Embrun P. O. is still in operation.

GIRVAN. Girvan might have become a lasting place name in Russell but for the sudden resignation of postmaster James Stevenson. In 1860, Stevenson named his office "Girvan" after a coastal town in Ayrshire, Scotland. (The name is drawn from the Gaelic *geàrr abhainn*, "the short river," the Water of Girvan being shorter than the neighboring River Stinchar.) I'd guess Stevenson must have been Scottish himself, as Girvan is only Scottish place-name found in this otherwise Irish and French county. Girvan P. O. lasted only two years until Stevenson's February 1862 resignation, when the name disappeared.

HURTUBISE. For a few years in the 1890s, Hurtubise was a rural post office in Cambridge Township. Hurtubise is a fairly rare French surname, and was the surname of the first (and only) postmaster, F.-N. Hurtubise. The office, which closed in September, 1895, is long forgotten, and its location is not precisely known. Hurtubise is pronounced "HER-chu-beez."

LIMOGES. With a population of about 1 100, Limoges is one of the larger villages in Russell County. The community grew up around the local railway station, which was originally known as simply "South Indian" from its location on South Indian Creek. The post office was also named South Indian when it opened in 1883. After World War I, local residents decided to change the community's name to something more distinctive. A final decision was made in 1926, when the post office was renamed "Limoges." While Limoges is a town in France, the Limoges being honored here was the pastor of surrounding St-Viateur parish, Rev. Honoré Limoges. The Reverend ministered to St-Viateur from 1913 until 1921. Limoges village is now just off Highway 417 in Cambridge Township.

LITHIA STATION. This name has disappeared from its original location, somewhere on the old New York Central Railway between Bourget and Pendleton. The station didn't even have a post office, so there's very little history to work with at Lithia. A possible source for the name is a community in Georgia called Lithia Springs—as often happened, this American place-name may have been transplanted to Eastern Ontario because of American participation in the local railway. Pana Station (see below) and Oconto Station (see Frontenac County) are both examples of American names coming into use here without any obvious local inspiration, other than their location on a railway funded by American backers. It's possible one of the New York Central's managers was from, or at least familiar with, Lithia Springs, GA.

NAVAN. Navan village is part of Cumberland Township. The village has grown in the last few years with the addition of new suburbs throughout Cumberland. Navan's name is another contribution from the area's Irish population: Navan town can be found in County Meath, near Dublin. The community's name means "the cave" (*An Uaimh*) in Irish Gaelic, and there are several caves in that part of Meath. Our Navan (pronounced "NAH-vun") was named in August, 1861.

ORIENT. Among the place-names of Russell, "Orient" stands out as one of the few not linked to a local family. Orient P. O. opened in Clarence Township in 1905, and managed to survive until 1918—by then, most of the small, pre-rural route offices had been axed. The name Orient probably originated from the office's location in eastern Clarence, though there is an Orient village in New York State.

PANA STATION. Pana Station, on the border between Russell Township and Gloucester Township in Carleton, has a highly unlikely name. The only other "Pana" seems to be a small town in Illinois—the name came from a chief of the Cahokia First Nation, who live in central Illinois. It's not clear how this obscure midwestern name could arrive in Russell, other than by the same route as Lithia (see above). A local source says Pana's last surviving building, the station house (which had been converted to a private residence), recently burnt down.

ST-ALBERT. Home of the popular St-Albert Cheese Factory, this village in Cambridge Township was named in 1876 after the local parish church. Apparently, the church was called St-Albert for the village curé, Albert Philion, *not* for either of the saints named Albert. The post office was granted as St-Albert in 1879.

ST-PASCHAL-BAYLON. Usually referred to as just "St-Pascal" [sic] by local residents, St-Paschal-Baylon is in Clarence Township. St-Paschal-Baylon was a Spaniard, born in the province of Aragon in 1540. He was a lay brother, leading an austere life and working to help the poor until his death in 1592. A post office opened under the name St-Paschal-Baylon in 1909, replacing an earlier office with the uninspiring name of "The Lake." After a four-year hiatus in the 1970s, St-Paschal-Baylon P. O. re-opened and is still in operation.

SARSFIELD. The name of this village in Cumberland has long eluded identification. It's highly likely that the "Sarsfield" meant here isn't a place, but an Irish soldier, Patrick Sarsfield. In 1690, when King William IV fought the famous Battle of the Boyne, Sarsfield was charged with defending the town of Limerick from the British forces. He led a spectacular defence of Limerick, which eventually was overcome by superior British numbers. Sarsfield's efforts are still remembered in Limerick Town, where an Irish military base is called Sarsfield Barracks. In 1874, Irish settlers in Cumberland probably had Patrick Sarsfield in mind when they named this community, now on Ottawa-Carleton Regional Road 28.

SOUTH NATION RIVER & VAL NATION. The South Nation is one of the largest rivers in Eastern Ontario. From its headwaters in a marsh near Brockville, the South Nation flows across the counties of Leeds, Grenville, Dundas, Stormont, Russell, and Prescott before emptying into the Ottawa near Wendover. The curious name (as there's no corresponding North Nation River) comes from the old French seigneury of Petite-Nation—it once occupied the land in Québec opposite the mouth of the South Nation. Petite-Nation was created in 1674, and over time passed into the hands of Louis-Joseph Papineau, leader of the 1838 patriote rebellions in Lower Canada. The town of Papineauville, in the former seigneury, is named for Petite-Nation's one-time owner. A Prescott County post office took the name "Val Nation" from its location on the river.

6. Carleton County

(Regional Municipality of Ottawa-Carleton)

Once a staunchly conservative farming county, Carleton has now become the bustling urban region of Ottawa-Carleton. In the 19th century, its population was overwhelmingly Irish—today, the region is the most multicultural in Eastern Ontario, with a large francophone population in Ottawa's eastern suburbs. Many of the old place-names in Carleton County have disappeared: the old townships were merged into a few large areas (with uninspired names like "West Carleton" and "Rideau"), and smaller villages are disappearing under urban sprawl. Fortunately, we're not so far away from the old place-names that they've been totally forgotten, and in the outlying areas of the region you can still find Irish names at virtually every four corners.

BALLINVILLA. This Irish name was once found in Nepean, near the intersection of Carling Avenue and the CN Railway line. From 1880 to 1891, Ballinvilla P. O. was located in the home of T. W. Kenny, an Irish farmer in what was then rural Nepean Township. The original Ballinvilla is a hamlet in Ireland's County Mayo, and was the birthplace of a settler (possibly Kenny himself) of our Ballinvilla. The hamlet's Gaelic name, *Baile an bhile*, means "the homestead of the old tree." Our Ballinvilla has not survived as a local street name—a regular occurrence where cities expand over older rural settlements—and, apparently, the name is no longer remembered in the area.

CARP. One of the larger rural towns in Ottawa-Carleton, Carp is now in the regionalized Township of West Carleton. (Pre-regionalization, Carp was in Huntley Township.) The village's name is no great mystery: Carp town was named for the Carp River, and the river was named for the fish. The name is only unusual because there is no other community in Canada (or at least no other populated place, according to the Census) whose name contains "Carp." There are dozens of Trout Lakes and Bass Lakes and Salmon Rivers, but there's only one Carp.

CATHARTIC / CARLSBAD SPRINGS. This oddly named community was the location of Eastman's Springs P. O., better known today as Carlsbad Springs. The community briefly boomed during the health spa craze of the late Victorian age (see Carratraca Springs under Prescott County). While Eastman's Springs and (from 1906) Carlsbad Springs were the approved post office names for the village, the local preference was Cathartic. Obviously, the name was given because of the beneficial (i.e., cathartic) effects ascribed to the hot springs. Cathartic frequently appeared on the maps in the late 1800s, but Carlsbad Springs is now the only recognized name for the community. Carlsbad Springs, incidentally, was the name of a well-known spa in Bohemia.

CLANDEBOYE / NAEV MEEHAL. These two names were applied in succession to a small rural post office in Huntley Township. Both names are Irish in origin, evidence of Huntley's overwhelming Irish population. Clandeboye comes from County Down, where Clandeboye House was the ancestral home of a Canadian governor-general, the Marquis of Dufferin and Ava. Naturally, Clandeboye P. O. opened in 1873, during Dufferin's term as our G-G. In Gaelic, the name is *Clann Aodha Buí*, "the descendants of Yellow Aodh," remembering a shadowy figure from ancient Irish history. The house is located in Crawfordsburn town, near the city of Bangor.

Naev Meehal is more complicated, requiring some imagination to see the Irish link. The name did not immediately replace Clandeboye—the post office became "McKinley P. O." in 1882, and stayed under that name until "Naev Meehal" was coined in 1909. The two words certainly look as if they might be Irish Gaelic, but really they only sound like Irish Gaelic. The clue lies in the first word, "Naev." The Gaelic word for "Saint" is *namh*, which is pronounced "nave" or, as it was spelled on this post office, "Naev." If Naev is simply a phonetic spelling of Saint, then the second word is probably "Michael"—in Gaelic, the name is pronounced just like "Meehal." Naev Meehal P. O., therefore, means St. Michael P. O. , a name undoubtedly inspired by the parish in which the post office was located, St. Michael's. This is still the name of the parish based in West Huntley, though Naev Meehal P. O. disappeared in 1918. It's unfortunate Naev Meehal hasn't survived, as it is not only a beautiful name but a clever invention of Naev Meehal's last postmaster.

CORKERY. This name was used for two different post offices in Huntley Township (now West Carleton Township). From 1906 to 1909, the community of West Huntley was called "Corkery P. O." In 1909, the name was transferred to a new post office, which remained open until 1967. The name came from the Barony of Corkeree, a title which conferred ownership of a large tract of land in County Westmeath. The Barony was called *Corca Raeidhe* in Gaelic, meaning "the people *(corca)* of Fiacha Raidhe." Fiacha Raidhe was a legendary Irish prince of the 2nd century a. d.

DUNROBIN. See Woodlawn-Dunrobin.

HAZELDEAN. The attractive name Hazeldean has been used for two different post offices in Goulbourn Township. The original Hazeldean P. O. was established in 1859, undoubtedly named for the village of Hazeldean in Scotland's Strathclyde region. That office closed during the introduction of rural home delivery in 1914. Years later, the area around the old Hazeldean had begun to suburbanize, and in 1969 a new Hazeldean P. O. was established to serve these new residents. The Hazeldean area was absorbed into the City of Kanata in the 1970s, and in 1975 Hazeldean P. O. was amalgamated with Ottawa. The old route of Highway 7 west of Ottawa is still called Hazeldean Road for this former farming hamlet.

JOCKVALE. The hamlet of Jockvale used to be a small farming community in southern Nepean Township. The hamlet has now been swallowed by Nepean's suburban development, and the name is most often seen today as a Nepean-area telephone exchange. "Jockvale" was coined in 1875 for a local post office—the hamlet is located near the Jock River, whose name is a corruption of the French Christian name "Jacques." Jockvale P. O. closed in 1926, though "Jockvale" survived in popular use long enough to be picked up by Bell Canada.

KARS. The name of this Rideau Township village sometimes provokes the question, "Does Kars have anything to do with cars?" Actually, when the name Kars was given to a post office here in September, 1856, cars hadn't even been invented. Like Odessa (see Lennox & Addington County) and Redan (see Leeds County), Kars remembers a battle from the Crimean War. In 1855, the Turkish town of Kars was defended by the British from Russian attack. However, by November of that year, the sustained Russian assault finally overpowered the British. To commemorate the battle, the community of Wellington (then in the pre-regional government Township of North Gower) decided to rename itself "Kars." The name Kars has also been given to a small township just northwest of Sault Ste. Marie.

MALAKOFF & WINDFALL. Malakoff village is located just north of Regional Road 6 in old Marlborough (now Rideau) Township. The name has a Slavic ring to it and, like nearby Kars, Malakoff can trace its name back to the Crimean War. Just east of the port city of Sevastapol, there is a tiny village called Malakoff —the Russians fought a major battle there against the invading British and

French. Sevastapol was eventually captured, and the people of Marlborough celebrated the victory by naming a post office here Malakoff in September 1856. Before the war, Malakoff was known locally as Windfall. Perhaps someone had found a windfall (a ripe apple blown from a tree) in or near the village during settlement.

MARCH. The angular Township of March has now been overrun by the City of Kanata, though at least a municipal ward in Kanata is still called "March Rural." The name was given in 1823 to honor Charles Lennox, a respected governor of Upper Canada (see Lennox & Addington County). The Earl of March was one of Lennox's titles, taken from the so-called Marches, or border areas, between England and Wales. The word goes back to an ancient English tribe, the Mercians, who controlled the Welsh border in the Dark Ages. Until 1913, a post office in March Township was called simply "March P. O."

MECHANICSVILLE. Modern Mechanicsville is a working-class neighbor-hood in the west end of Ottawa, but the community originally started as a rural milling town. As historian Bruce Elliott has recorded, Mechanicsville was created in 1872 to house workers at the Little Chaudière Mills. The presence of these millworkers inspired the name "Mechanicsville" for the post office, which opened in 1887. Mechanicsville suffered heavily when the mills were shut down, the post office closing in 1918 from lack of business. Eventually, the village was annexed to Ottawa. You can now find Mechanicsville at the north end of Parkdale Avenue.

THE MER BLEUE. This large marsh covers a substantial part of Gloucester and neighboring Cumberland Township. The name means "the blue sea" in French, and was given because the marsh was always severely flooded. The Mer Bleue has survived encroaching suburban development so far, and is still the source for several local creeks.

NAEV MEEHAL. See Clandeboye.

TORBOLTON. In contrast to the heavily Irish character of most Carleton place names, the Township of Torbolton—now part of West Carleton Township—traces its name to a church parish in Scotland. Torbolton was found among the titles of the Duke of Richmond (see Lennox & Addington County) who was "Baron Settrington and Methuen of Torbolton." Richmond's name and titles were used all over Eastern Ontario as place names (at March, for example). The original Scottish parish is called Tarbolton, and is well known to readers of Robbie Burns as Burns' birthplace. The change from "a" in Tarbolton to "o" in

Torbolton was probably caused by a slip in pronunciation between the two sides of the Atlantic. Torbolton Township was established in 1823.

VARS. One of Carleton's more unusual names, Vars (pronounced as it's written, "VARZ") was originally known simply as Bear Brook Station. The station is now gone, and the brook has become Shaws Creek since the 19th century. (The change from Bear Brook Station to Vars occurred in 1886.) The traditional story of Vars' name is that the local vicar, Fr. Guillaume, suggested the name after his birthplace in France. Additionally, the name may have been inspired in part because our Vars and the village of Embrun (see Russell County) are almost the same distance apart as the French villages of Vars and Embrun.

WINDFALL. See Malakoff.

WOODLAWN-DUNROBIN. These two villages in West Carleton Township now go under the unified postal name of Woodlawn-Dunrobin. Of the two, Dunrobin was named first—the post office opened there in 1870, some ten years before Woodlawn P. O. The name Dunrobin comes from a Scottish castle, once the ancestral seat of the powerful Sutherland family. The old county in which the castle stood, Sutherlandshire, was named for them. Dunrobin means "the fortress (*dun*) of Robert (*robin*)," Robert Sutherland being one of the earliest known members of the Sutherland family. (He lived during the latter half of the 13th century.) The first postmaster at Dunrobin, Henry Younghusband, traced his roots to Sutherlandshire as well. Younghusband's mother was born near the ancient castle.

As for Woodlawn, its name probably comes from one of several American Woodlawns. (I couldn't find an inhabited place called "Woodlawn" in the U. K.) Woodlawn P. O. opened in the era of the post office's American name list (see Little Britain under Victoria County), so the government may have assigned "Woodlawn" from that list.

7. Grenville County

For most of its existence, Grenville County has been joined with its larger western neighbor, Leeds. During the late 18th century, the community of Johnstown in Edwardsburgh Township was planned as the administrative centre for Eastern Ontario. For a brief time the tiny village filled that role, but it was quickly overshadowed and today has almost entirely disappeared. The place names of Grenville resemble those of Dundas, the townships and larger communities having English names while the smaller villages being more Irish. The progenitor of the Dundas name would also have known the "Grenville" of Grenville County—William Wyndham Grenville was a Speaker of the English House of Commons and a cabinet colleague of Henry Dundas. Grenville later became Britain's prime minister in 1806.

BLUE CHURCH ROAD. The Blue Church Road, now Leeds & Grenville Road 31, crosses Highway 401 a few kilometres west of Prescott. Blue Church hamlet is at the foot of the road where it meets Highway 2. Unlike The Island (see below), the name Blue Church means exactly what it says—the village is graced by a unique blue church, built in 1845 and now a historic site. A post office called Blue Church Road opened in Augusta Township in 1906, but was closed down only seven years later. The community was once known as New Oswegatchie, after Fort Oswegatchie (now Oswego) in northern New York State. In Iroquois, Oswegatchie means something like "the mouth of the black river."

FARMERS UNION. This odd name was briefly used for a post office in Oxford-on-Rideau Township. From 1907 to 1913, the office operated about seven kilometres north of the village of Merrickville. The name "Farmers Union" was taken from the local cheese factory—as the factory was run by a co-operative, "Farmers Union" was simply a description of the factory's operation. Farmers Union wasn't around long enough to become a recognized place-name, and is no longer in use.

GARRYOWEN. At first blush this old community name from Edwardsburgh looks like a personal name (i.e., "Garry Owen"). The hamlet, which lies just northeast of Spencerville, is really named for a small Irish village in County Limerick. The "Owen" of the name *is* a personal name, but the "Garry" is a corruption of the Gaelic word *garradha*, "garden." "Garryowen" is, therefore, "the Garden of Owen."

GLEN SMAIL. Glen Smail (pronounced SMAYL) hamlet is located just off Highway 16 in Edwardsburgh Township. In 1878, Glen Smail P. O. opened on Edwardsburgh's 5th Line, and continued to operate there until 1913. The office took its name from a local settler, William Smail, whose descendants can still be found in the Spencerville area. As with Cashion's Glen (see Glengarry County) and many other post offices in the easternmost counties of Ontario, "Glen" was used here instead of "-ville" or "corners" to invent a name for this post office.

GOWER, SOUTH. South Gower (pronounced GOAR), and its now-vanished counterpart North Gower, were two oddly shaped townships created in 1798 along the Rideau. They took up an angular gap needed to make all the townships around them line up square. North Gower was absorbed into Rideau Township when regional government came to Carleton County—South Gower survives in Grenville as one of the smallest townships in Ontario.

There are two conflicting stories about the name "Gower." One, which you often hear locally, says Gower comes from the surveying term "gore." A gore is an irregular slice of land, used by a surveyor to make one township line up exactly with a neighboring township. This was frequently necessary, as the earliest townships were often created as perfectly square as possible without regard to the lay of the land. To make new townships square as well (and to make them fit within the predetermined county boundaries), gores had to be put in place to compensate for odd angles. This is precisely why North & South Gower were created—to make neat, square townships around the Rideau, two "gore" townships were required.

The second story, which is the "official" version, says the townships were named for Admiral John Gower, 2nd Earl of Gower and commander of the English forces at Québec in 1782. The Gowers took their title from the Welsh town of Gower—the name comes from the Welsh word *gwyr*, "a curved promontory." A riding in southeastern Wales is now known as "Gower."

THE ISLAND. This railway whistle-stop in Edwardsburgh Township seems to have a completely nonsensical name—The Island is not on, and is nowhere near, an island! The hamlet is between a large marsh and the South Nation River, but hardly surrounded by water. Given that Grenville had a substantial Irish population at one time, it's possible The Island takes its name from one of two Irish locations. In County Dublin, a short distance west of Dublin city, is a little four-corners called The Island. Like our Edwardsburgh village, this Irish community is also inland. Another possibility is a small street in the town of Limerick, which is known simply as "The Island." It may seem far-fetched for a Limerick street name to end up in this community. However, other street names have been used in much larger communities in Eastern Ontario, the most conspicuous of which is Carleton Place (from a square in Glasgow). Of course, maybe the Irish farmers of Edwardsburgh were just thinking of the island of Ireland.

JASPER. This is one of Eastern Ontario's most elusive place-names. Originally known as Irish Creek, from the large Irish population in the area, Jasper's "Jasper" has remained unidentified for more than a century. If there's a significant Irish Jasper, he or she can't be that significant! The only lead we have is an American soldier, William Jasper, for whom a half-dozen towns in the United States are named. Jasper was killed in 1779 during the American Revolution, and in honor of his (brief, it seems) military career, communities across the eastern U.S. called themselves "Jasper." With Grenville's close connections to Upper New York State, it's possible the name crossed the St. Lawrence and was used here in 1864. At one time, this village was also known as "Albune," a baffling and rootless name to date.

KILMARNOCK. Standing at a sharp bend in the Rideau River, Kilmarnock village falls partly in Grenville's Wolford Township and partly in Lanark's Township of Montague. The village has one of the few Scottish place-names found in Grenville—the original town of Kilmarnock is about thirty kilometers southwest of Glasgow. In Gaelic, Kilmarnock means the "Church of St. Ernan," remembering a disciple of the early Christian missionary St. Columba. Readers of Robbie Burns will undoubtedly know the Scottish Kilmarnock, as the official Burns Museum has been established there. Perhaps a Burns fan was responsible for naming our Kilmarnock, which came into official use as a post office name in 1829.

MILD VIEW. Mild View Post Office was hardly open in 1909 before it was shut down in 1913. The office operated at Newmanville hamlet, and today only Newmanville is shown on the maps. Mild View was probably given to reflect the landscape of Oxford-on-Rideau Township, which is low-lying and still dotted with farms.

WOLFORD CHAPEL. The original Wolford Chapel is in England, and is the burial place of Upper Canada's first governor, John Graves Simcoe. His family estate is also known as Wolford, and its name was given to this Grenville township. Most of the townships in this area were named during Simcoe's tenure (1791-1796), and can trace their names to either Simcoe himself or his close friends.

YULE. Tiny Yule hamlet lies in Wolford Township, right on the boundary between Grenville and Leeds Counties. The name may have been given in Christmas cheer, but Yule is most likely Irish in origin. In County Cork, there is a town called Youghal whose name is pronounced like the English word "yule." Youghal comes from the Gaelic word eochaill, meaning "yew wood"—the yew is a fairly common tree in parts of Ireland. Many other place-names from Cork have also found their way to Eastern Ontario, including Cloyne (see Lennox & Addington County) and Fermoy (see Frontenac County).

8. Leeds County

Leeds County is home to the famous Thousand Islands, a popular holiday spot for more than a century. The hundreds of islands there have a remarkable variety of place-names, reflecting not only Canada's military history, but also the creativity (or even quirkiness!) of its inhabitants. While the front concessions of the Leeds mainland were settled by the Loyalists, Famine Irish are the largest ethnic group in the county's population. Irish names can be found in every township, with a few Scottish and English contributions. Leeds County honors another British cabinet minister, Francis Godolphin Osborne, the 3rd Duke of Leeds. Osborne was briefly home secretary during the fly-by-night government of Lord Shelburne (1782-83).

ANOMA LEA. Despite its small size, this community has had more names than almost any other single community in Eastern Ontario. The hamlet, which is on Leeds Road 30 in the Rear of Yonge & Escott, has been called Alguires Corners, Coons Corners, Cughans Corners, Pattemores Corners, and Addison Road. The final choice of Anoma Lea was made in the 1890s by the local school-teacher, Mrs. C. Howe. Perhaps stumped for a definitive choice, Mrs. Howe noted the community's unremarkable countryside and called it the "no-name meadow" in Latin—Anoma Lea. Another old tale says Anoma Lea was an anagram, composed of the first letter of the Christian name of each member of the women's institute. (Inventive!) Unfortunately, all this naming effort has been largely forgotten, as "Anoma Lea" is seldom recognized in Leeds today.

BALLYCANOE. The name of this hamlet in Front of Yonge is a play on words: while the pioneers of Leeds spent a lot of time travelling the county in canoes, the Wexford Irish among them would have been well acquainted with a hamlet in the "Old Country" called Ballycanew. Ballycanew is located just north of Cahore Point, another Wexford place name that migrated to Canada with the Famine Irish (see Stormont County). The "-canoe" spelling might have been accidental, but the word play is too obvious to overlook.

BASTARD. The Township of Bastard easily wins the prize for having the ugliest name of any township in Ontario! Naturally, plenty of stories have grown up around how this attention-grabbing name was given to the township. One story says "Bastard" came about by accident. A leading citizen of the township had been sent to Toronto to tell the government which name the citizens had chosen for their municipality. When the elder arrived, he was too embarrassed to say the approved choice, "Stevenstown," because the name was given in honor of him. An exasperated clerk, searching for something to put in his records, asked the elder, "Well, sir, who is the father of the community?" "We don't really have one," said the shy farmer. "Well, then, it's a bastard township," said the clerk, and wrote "Bastard" into the books.

The real story of Bastard's name is less entertaining. Bastard was the surname of a wealthy English family who were personal friends of Upper Canada's governor, John Graves Simcoe. When this township was being surveyed, a John Polloxfen Bastard was a British MP representing Simcoe's home riding in England, Honiton. At Simcoe's instructions, this township was named for John Bastard, and immediately stories began to circulate among the settlers about the bizarre name of their new home. There have been several attempts to change the name of "Bastard"—another is under way at the time of writing. It would be a shame to lose one of the classic place-names of Eastern Ontario.

CHAFFEYS LOCKS. The fairly straightforward name of this Rideau Canal village has been debated by the provincial government and local residents for years. The origin is not in doubt: Sam and Ben Chaffey were millwrights who owned a series of mills along the Rideau, including one in the village that bears their name. The argument is about how to spell the name. The provincial government says it's "Chaffeys Locks"—the village insists it should be "Chaffey's Lock." The problem arose because, early in this century, the provincial government decreed all apostrophes were to be stricken from Ontario place-names. (Really!) Under this policy, Smith's Falls became Smiths Falls, Colpoy's Bay became Colpoys Bay, and Chaffey's Lock became Chaffeys Lock. Then, many people in the Rideau system got into the habit of using "Chaffeys Locks," even though, as the villagers point out, there is only one lock here. For some reason, the official post office name, given in 1880, has always been in the plural. (There's no longer a post office in town, but Chaffeys Locks is still a valid address and postal code.) So now the village is fighting to get its apostrophe back and to change "Locks" back to just plain "Lock." The province eventually relented on its apostrophe policy, but so far the government simply won't call a lock a lock.

THE DEVIL'S DOOR ROAD. This quiet side-road in the Front of Yonge shows good humor on someone's part. The road forms the main intersection at Yonge Mills, and right at the centre of Yonge Mills is the 1837 Stone Church. (The attractive building is now one of the oldest surviving churches in Eastern Ontario.) As you step out the door of the church, your first steps are on the Devil's Door Road!

FIDDLER'S ELBOW. The Fiddler's Elbow is a narrow channel in the Navy Group of the Thousand Islands. Apparently, the name does not refer to the shape of the channel, but to an actual fiddler—he often played at this spot for the passing tourists.

FORFAR. Well known for its cheese factory, Forfar hamlet is on Highway 42 in Bastard Township. Surprisingly, given its fair size, Forfar hasn't had a post office since 1970—the name certainly hasn't lost any of its profile in the meantime. The original town of Forfar is in Scotland, where one of the old counties was also called Forfarshire. (The county was more often known as Angusshire before it was abolished in the 1970s.) The meaning of the name "Forfar" is not settled—it's been given as "a wooded ridge" and as "the spying hill," depending on how you interpret the name's elements in Gaelic.

FURNACE FALLS. See Lyndhurst.

GLEN ELBE. This tiny village on Elbe Creek has gone through a bewildering series of name changes in its history. In 1857, a post office was granted for this location in the Rear of Yonge & Escott under the name "Elbe." (The name comes from a large German river.) In 1862, Elbe closed, but nine years later the office was reopened under the name "Dickens." In 1885, Dickens was scrapped in favor of the seemingly erroneous "Elb Mills." Maybe the "e" was dropped by a record-keeper at the post office department. The name Elb Mills set a record here, lasting thirty years until yet another change, this time to "Glen Elbe." In 1913, this post office was finally closed, leaving Glen Elbe as the name to be passed down to us. The hamlet now consists of only a few houses clustered around little Elbe Creek.

IVY LEA. One of the most widely recognized place-names in Eastern Ontario is Ivy Lea. The bridge connecting Ontario to northern New York State is called the "Ivy Lea Bridge" after the little hamlet near its Canadian entrance. The community of Ivy Lea, just off the Thousand Islands Parkway, is a residential hamlet which once boasted a popular hotel. Both the hotel, called the Ivy Lea, and the post office—which opened in 1887—were named for the local Ivey family. John Ivey was the first postmaster at the hamlet, and he coined the name

"Ivy Lea" from his own surname and the hamlet's riverside location. (Ivey confirmed this was the source of Ivy Lea in a 1909 letter.) The post office closed in 1927, and the hotel has gone out of business, but the name is still synonymous with summering in the Thousand Islands.

JELLYBY. This name of this hamlet in Elizabethtown Township tends to make people do a double take. Jellyby, also known as Jelly or Jelly's Crossing, is not the dessert capital of Eastern Ontario but an old railway whistle-stop. When the line was constructed, it crossed the property of one Andrew Jelly—as often happened, the station or stop placed on Jelly's property was named for him.

KALARIA ISLAND. Also known as Blackberry Island, Kalaria is said to have been named by its one-time owner, a Mr. Castle. He was an instructor in Greek, and chose "Kalaria" (meaning "fair winds") from that language.

LAKE ELOIDA (LOYADA). The long-disputed name of this attractive lake can be traced to the area's first settler. In 1804, land along the lake was granted to Elaida Parish, who later served as quartermaster to the Leeds Militia's 2nd Regiment. Other sources claim Parish was a member of the party that surveyed the rear of Yonge and Escott Townships in 1811. The story becomes more complicated, because in the 19th century the lake was regularly referred to as Lake Loyada. It's possible "Loyada" could be a corrupted form of "Elaida"— Elaida is such an unusual Christian name it could easily be garbled or mistaken when passed down orally. There is a place called "Loyada" in Africa, but there's no obvious way this obscure name could have ended up in Leeds.

In this century, a long argument ensued over whether the lake should be Loyada or Eloida. The question wasn't even settled when an "Eloida P. O." was approved for the area in 1906. Only a ruling by the Federal Names Secretariat finally gave the nod to Eloida. The name is pronounced "el-OY-duh."

THE LAKE FLEET ISLANDS. The Lake Fleet is a group of small, rocky islands located east of Gananoque. Each of the islands takes its name from a 19th century sailing ship—the ships saw action in the War of 1812, or were used in the survey of the Thousand Islands. Among the Lake Fleets are *Deathdealer Island, Dumbfounder Island, Bloodletter Island, Belabourer Island, Endymion Island* (part of Thousand Islands National Park), *Psyche Island, Astounder Island,* and *Axeman Island.*

LYN. Lyn village near Brockville has one of the shortest place-names in Eastern Ontario. Its only competitors are the Townships of Oso (see Frontenac County) and Ops (see Victoria County), and the hamlet of Ida near Peterborough. The name Lyn was brought here by Loyalists from Massachusetts, where there is also a town called "Lyn." Both Lyns originate in the Scottish Gaelic word *lyne*, meaning "a stream or pool." Appropriately, our Lyn is situated on a stream, Lyn Creek. Lyn P. O. is one of the county's oldest, now at 143 years of continuous service and counting.

LYNDHURST & FURNACE FALLS. This village, located about half-way between Highways 15 and 42, has its origins in Ontario's first iron forge. In the 1790s, a forge was constructed here to serve the nearby farmers, many of whom had just arrived in the isolated shield country. The forge was quickly overtaken by other blacksmiths in the area, and even in the early 1800s one observer described these iron works as "a ruin." In the 1830s, though, one local resident remembered the old forge and called a new post office in this area "Furnace Falls." The office didn't last long, but the name is still known in the township. (Apparently, there is no connection between this village and another Furnace Falls near Minden [see Haliburton County].) In 1851, a second post office was granted in the area of old Furnace Falls. Called Lyndhurst for a community in Hampshire, England, the office's name means "the lime-tree hill" in Old English. The English Lyndhurst was the birthplace of a Canadian governor, Sir John Colborne.

MUDLUNTA ISLAND. Part of the Admiralties—an island group facing Gananoque—Mudlunta is said to be a Mississauga word meaning "half-moon." The island is also called Barrow's Island for a British military officer, Sir John Barrow.

NAUVOO (ELGIN). This curious name was once applied to Elgin, a police village on Highway 15 in South Crosby. (Police villages are councils set up to provide basic services to villages too small to be officially incorporated.) Elgin is almost unique in Eastern Ontario, as it was originally settled by a party of Mormons. The word "nauvoo," said to mean "beautiful," was taken from a town in Utah to name this village. A few years after the village was founded, virtually the entire Mormon congregation left Nauvoo and headed for the American Mid-west. The name Nauvoo was then abandoned in favor of "Elgin," for Canadian governor Lord Elgin.

PLUM HOLLOW. This village is one of the most attractive in Leeds, situated on a steep hillside overlooking the farmland of Bastard Township. Plum Hollow's location inspired the name—when the Loyalist settlers arrived here, they found a grove of wild plum trees in the hollow below the hill. The name "Plum Hollow" took root and has been in official use since the post office opened in May 1863. The village was long home to a local cheese factory that has now shut its doors.

POONAMALIE LOCKS. These are the final set of locks on the Rideau Canal before the town of Smiths Falls. The unusual name sounds East Indian, and it is—Poonamalie is a town in India, near Bombay (which is known as Mumbey today.) A British military officer christened the locks Poonamalie because they reminded him of the Indian town. The cedars lining the locks resembled a particular location in Poonamalie, so the story goes. The road leading into the lock station is also called Poonamalie.

REDAN. Redan village is near Brockville in Elizabethtown Township. In a round-about way, the names comes from the Crimean War. In the late 1800s, area residents met to choose a name for their new school section. They couldn't come to a decision, and, as often happened (see Buckshot under Frontenac County, for example), this discussion quickly turned into an argument. When she had a chance to speak, the local schoolteacher quoted the assembly the following lines: "At the Crimean War, the dark redan in silence calls/Grim and threatening . . ." (A "redan" is a military fortification.) She compared the argument over the name to the battles of the Crimea. The crowd agreed that this was an argument worth remembering, so they called the school section "Redan" from the lines of the poem! The name was picked up for the community post office in 1911.

TINCAP. The village of Tincap is now largely a residential satellite of Brockville. During the 19th century, however, Tincap was a thriving rural village in Elizabethtown Township. In 1882, a post office with the unremarkable name of Spring Valley had been granted in this vicinity. However, by 1912, it was decided to move the office a short distance down the road, where there was a much busier intersection. (The name Spring Valley is still used for the area just north of Tincap.) The newly appointed postmaster was asked to come up with a new name for his office. As he sat mulling over the request, he looked out the window and saw the shiny tin cupola on the village schoolhouse. Inspired, he immediately wrote down "Tincap." Tincap P. O. remained open until 1948. Unfortunately, the schoolhouse that inspired the name no longer exists.

TONIATA. "Toniata" is an ancient aboriginal name which is no longer used in Leeds. Toniata Island and Toniata River were names employed by the French in the 17th century—as Percy Robinson writes, "The former is now known as Grenadier Island and the latter with prosaic bathos has descended to Jones

Creek. It is to be regretted that so euphonious a name as Toniata has disappeared and with it a good deal of local history." The original Toniata was a village, possibly of Algonquin people, on Grenadier Island. The village was abandoned some time in the 1640s, but the name continued to be used for the remainder of the French regime. When the British first mapped the Thousand Islands, surveyor Sir Michael Owen abandoned "Toniata" in both its former locations. According to Robinson, the word *toniata*, meaning simply "a point of land," was found in the Huron and Iroquois languages.

YNYSCRAG ISLAND. First called simply Island 25, Ynyscrag has a Welsh name describing the island's appearance. Translated from Welsh, "ynys crag" means "rocky island."

9. Lanark County

As its Highland name might suggest, Lanark received thousands of Scottish settlers in the 19th century. Like Glengarry, Lanark is proud of its nearly two centuries of Scottish heritage. The township names of Lanark aren't particularly Scottish, but the community names are practically a road-map of central Scotland. The old Scottish county of Lanarkshire (now absorbed into the administrative Region of Strathclyde) was home to many early settlers of our Lanark, as was Perthshire, remembered in the Canadian Lanark's county town. The word "lanark" has been traced back to the language of the Picts, a mysterious people who lived in Scotland before the ancestors of the modern Scots arrived. While this is only an educated guess on the part of historians, "lanerc" in Pictish probably meant "a glade."

ARKLAN. Arklan is an obscure post office name from the Township of Lanark. The office was run from the home of Thomas Young from 1905 until the start of the First World War. The name might have a genuine relative in Scotland (there are a number of villages called Arkland in Dumfries & Galloway Region), but "Arklan" is really an anagram of "Lanark." Just reverse the syllables.

CLYDE FORKS. This name was given to a station on the old Kick & Push Railway in 1930. The station had been there for about forty years before, but until 1930 the community was known as "Caldwell's Mills" for mill owner Boyd Caldwell. The name Clyde Forks was coined because the village is at a fork in the Clyde River—at the time, the Clyde was a key transportation route in northwestern Lanark, and was often jammed with timber rafts after spring break-up. (Not surprisingly, the Clyde is named for a major river in central Scotland.) Both the post office and the railway station are gone, but Clyde Forks is still very much alive.

THE CUCKOO'S NEST. This strange place-name is used for an area in southeastern Beckwith Township, reached by a township road known as the "Cuckoo's Nest Road." The name Cuckoo's Nest may go back to the first European settlement of Beckwith, around 1820. Though they are not very common, two kinds of cuckoos (the black-billed and yellow-billed) are found in Ontario, and the presence of an actual cuckoo's nest may have inspired the choice. The name still survives in local usage and tradition in Beckwith.

THE DERRY. Running from the Jock River marsh through to Beckwith's eastern boundary, the Derry is a farming area first settled by Irish immigrants around 1820. The people chose the name Derry (from the Gaelic *doire*, "oak grove") to describe their new home in heavily forested Lanark County. A few of the original families, like the Kidds, can still be found along the Fifth and Sixth Lines of Beckwith.

ELPHIN. Elphin is the only village in tiny North Sherbrooke Township, united with Lavant and Dalhousie for local government purposes. The village, like the rest of Lanark, was settled almost exclusively by Scots during the 1820s and 1830s. The community of Elphin chose its current name in 1860, in honor of a wealthy Scottish family, the Elphinstones. The Lords of Elphinstone were powerful nobles in Scotland, controlling a large estate they'd owned since the Middle Ages. The Elphinstones had been around for so long that one of the communities they owned, Elphin village, had borne their name for centuries. In 1860, John, the 13th Lord of Elphinstone, had just been given a new English title. In honor of the occasion, his countrymen in North Sherbrooke picked "Elphin" for their new post office.

FLOWER STATION. This isolated hamlet was the northernmost Kick & Push Railway station in Lanark County. The community is still there, complete with general store, some thirty years after the railway was dismantled. The attractive name "Flower Station" comes from the Flower family of New York State—the Flowers invested heavily in the railway and played leading roles in the company. R. P. Flower was the K & P's general manager at one time, and he personally oversaw construction of this section of the railway. Flower Station still had its post office until 1969.

FOLGER STATION & MOPEVILLE. Folger Station is a former Kick & Push community that has only just survived the railway's disappearance. A few homes still stand at the station site, which is down a long, rugged side-road from Canonto (see Frontenac County). The community, which was named for K & P director B. W. Folger, survived on forestry until the timber was exhausted. The post office left town in 1928, and most of the residents followed suit. Folger is best remembered as the site of a terrible wreck in 1917—the engine derailed in a wash-out, killing the engineer and injuring several passengers.

Near Folger, there was a dead-end siding which was dubbed Mopeville. Cars could often run right off the tracks at Mopeville, which probably accounted for the name. The enormous effort required to drag the cars back onto the line was guaranteed to create plenty of long, tired faces!

GRANNY CUMMING'S CORNER (WATSONS CORNERS). The community now known as Watsons Corners originally started life with the more unusual name of Granny Cumming's Corner. Granny Cumming was an elderly Scottish settler who arrived in Dalhousie Township about 1820. She came with her children and grandchildren in tow—one of those descendants, Peter Cumming, is remembered as the one-time librarian of the Dalhousie Library. (The library, established in 1828, is the oldest rural public library in the province.)

As the village grew around the main intersection (now at County Road 8 and the Dalhousie 3rd Line), the name Watsons Corners also came into use. The Watsons were another prominent Scottish family, and in 1852 the post office was named "Watsons Corners" for them. Watsons Corners P. O. was shut down exactly one hundred years later, in 1952. Since then, Watsons Corners has also become the "Kangaroo Capital of Canada." When you're in town, stop and ask about it!

LAMMERMOOR. This isolated hamlet in Dalhousie Township probably takes its name from a novel by Sir Walter Scott. *The Bride of Lammermoor* (published in 1819) tells of a noble Scotswoman, Lucy Ashton, forced to break off a promised engagement to her lover. Her father then forces her to marry another man. She is so grief-stricken by this arranged marriage that she goes mad, tries to kill her husband, and dies shortly afterward. The story does take its name from a real place in Scotland—Lammermoor, or "Lammermuir" as it is usually spelled today, is a hilly, unpopulated area southeast of Edinburgh. The word *Lammermuir* means "the lamb's moor" in Middle English. The almost-uniformly Scottish population here would have known both the novel and the original Lammermoor.

LAVANT. This rugged township in Lanark's northwestern corner is home to many of the county's most interesting place-names, including Flower Station and Clyde Forks. The township itself takes its name from a small community in southeastern England—the village of Lavant was part of, or near, the estate of Canadian Governor Charles Lennox. Names associated with Lennox are sprinkled all over Eastern Ontario (see Lennox & Addington County, for example), and any connection with the governor was sufficient cause to put a place-name here. An old story that Lavant was a French trapper in northwestern Lanark is unsubstantiated.

The name "Lavant" (usually pronounced with the emphasis on the second syllable, i.e., "lah-VANT") has a particular meaning in southeastern England. In Kent, Sussex, and other neighboring counties, a "lavant" is a seasonal or shallow stream. There are a number of small streams and rivers in England all named "the Lavant" from this word. The village which gave its name to our township is on one of these Lavant streams.

Two communities in the township have also taken the name Lavant. Lavant village, which has acquired some recent monster homes, is at the eastern end of Robertson Lake. There is also a Lavant Station some three kilometers west of Robertson Lake. The village's half-dozen or so homes still line the old K & P right-of-way, as does the former Lavant Memorial Church. Lavant Station P. O. opened in 1883, and lasted until 1969.

LODORE. This old post office name is no longer recognized in Dalhousie Township. The office was at a remote intersection on Dalhousie's 7th line, about half-way between Horne Lake and Patterson Lake. A recent topographic map shows only one lonely building in the area. Lodore P. O., which closed in 1928, has been recorded as "Ladore" and "Ledore." However, the source of the name —Lodore Falls in Cumbria, England—shows the proper spelling. The falls are on a river called the Derwent Water.

MICAVILLE (STANLEYVILLE). The gold-colored mineral mica, used to manufacture lubricants, is plentiful in the shield country of Eastern Ontario. A number of large mica mines once operated here, including one in Lanark's North Burgess Township. The community is now called Stanleyville, after the local Stanley family, but from 1900 to 1912 the post office went by "Micaville." The village was settled back in the 1860s, when it was known as Hamlet. (It's not clear if this name was simply descriptive or taken from Shakespeare!) Stanleyville became the official name in 1879, but the discovery of mica prompted the temporary change to Micaville. The former mine site is now part of Murphys Point Provincial Park.

MOPEVILLE. See Folger Station.

NUMOGATE. Numogate village, on Highway 15, owes its name to the creativity of the first postmaster. He originally suggested "Montague P. O.," after the local township, but there was already a Montague Post Office here. Stumped for an alternative, he took the letters of "Montague" and toyed with them until he came up with the anagram "Numogate." The name is usually said "NEW-mow-gate." Incidentally, when Numogate came into being, Montague sounded very different than it does today. While the township is known as "MAWN-ta-gew" to us, in the 19th century the pronunciation was "MAWN-tag."

OCHIL. Ochil (pronounced "oh-KILL") was briefly a post office name in northern Lavant Township. The office may have been somewhere near the turn for Clyde Forks, but we can't be certain. The name of Ochil would have been familiar to the Scottish settlers here—back in the "old country," the Ochill (with two "ll"s) Hills run along the border between England and Scotland. Ochill has been tentatively traced back to an ancient British Celtic word meaning "high," the Ochills then being "the high ones." The Celts may have worshipped or feared these hills, and the description "the high ones" conveys this reverence. The steep hills of Lavant undoubtedly brought back memories of the looming Ochills.

POLAND. Poland is a sleepy little village on Lanark Road 14, just where 14 crosses the 3rd Line of Dalhousie. The village still has its venerable insulbrick church and its general store, which is fairly remarkable given Poland's size. The source of "Poland" is obvious, but why the name Poland was chosen is hotly disputed. Tradition says Poland was suggested to postmaster Moses Paul by his brother, but—unfortunately—Paul didn't record what the rationale was. In the 1800s there was a hotel in town called the Warsaw, but it's not clear if it was called the Warsaw from its location in Poland, or whether Poland might have been inspired by the Warsaw. One story says the village was called Poland because it was on Moses Paul's land . . . i.e., "Paul's land," Pol-and. Something like that.

Someone else suggested that getting to Poland was like trying to get to the north pole, thus "pole-land." (Getting here in February is no treat, but it's hardly *that* bad!) Yet another explanation is that there were plenty of poles (but definitely no Poles) cut from the timber here during settlement, so a different kind of "pole-land." There are probably other stories, too, though I'm tempted to believe that the Pauls simply pulled Poland out of the newspaper. The country was frequently in the news during the 1800s, as the Poles repeatedly rebelled against enforced Russian rule. One of these uprisings might have occurred in 1860, when Poland P. O. was named. Any takers?!

ROSETTA. The hamlet of Rosetta, in central Lanark Township, can probably trace its name to Rosetta, Egypt, where the world-famous Rosetta Stone was discovered. The stone was still renowned years after its discovery, and may have inspired the name of this village's post office in 1854. Local residents point out that our Rosetta also has an important stone of its own—before there was a church in the village, religious services were held outdoors, with the minister speaking from the top of a rocky outcrop. Local residents called it the Preaching Stone, and a creative settler may have thought of this as his or her own religious Rosetta. (It's a reach, but it's possible, isn't it?!)

UNEEDA. This disused post office name from Pakenham Township seems to say "you need a" something! This is the traditional explanation of the name— someone suggested "you need a post office," and when the office was named in 1905, the postmaster (maybe only half-seriously) put down "Uneeda." Another possibility is that the office was named after Uneeda, West Virginia, established in 1898. That Uneeda also has a "you need a post office" story!

WEMYSS. Wemyss (pronounced "WEAM-iss") is on Highway 7 in Bathurst Township, half-way between Perth and Maberly. The name was approved for a Bathurst post office in 1887. The choice has been described as a nod to a Scottish noble, Lord Wemyss. His title must have come from Wemyss Bay, a coastal bay separating the Scottish mainland from the Cowal Peninsula. The bay is part of the Firth of Clyde, another Scottish place-name which has immigrated to Lanark County (see Clyde Forks, above). Wemyss is an odd combination of the Gaelic word *uaimh* ("cave") and the English plural ending "-s."

WILBUR STATION. This lively mining town was between Snow Road Station (see Frontenac County) and Lavant Station (see above) on the Kick & Push. Iron was the only game in town, and the community thrived as long as the local mines were in operation. Wilbur suffered a major setback when the Great Vennachar Fire (see Lennox & Addington County) roared through in 1903, "wiping the village from the map" in the words of one local newspaper. The community declined after the 1920s, and has almost been reclaimed by the bush. One Dr. Wilbur was associated with the Bethlehem Iron Mining Co., which owned the local mine, and his name was given to the station around 1886.

10. Renfrew County

If you've driven a "fer wey" up from Ottawa, you know you've reached Renfrew County. In terms of size, Renfrew is the largest county in Eastern Ontario, including all the land between Algonquin Park and the wide Ottawa River—thirty-four townships in total. This is the frontier of Eastern Ontario, where lumber was (and often still is) the only employer in town. The seemingly never-ending supply of timber brought a similarly bottomless supply of tycoons, and their businesses spawned the city of Pembroke and dozens of smaller settlements. In the 19th century, the Opeongo Colonization Road was cut from the Ottawa River right across Renfrew to the edge of Algonquin, allowing settlers access to the wild county interior. The Opeongo brought not just settlers from the U.K., but also groups of central Europeans—Germans, Poles, and German-speaking Kaszubs all made their way up the muddy Opeongo Line to found new communities. As a result of this varied immigration, Renfrew's place-names are unique among the counties of Eastern Ontario.

ASHDAD. There's not much left of Ashdad any more, but the distinctive name is still well known in the Valley. The community was created by the Kick & Push Railway, which decided to put a station between Calabogie and the Opeongo Line. The name Ashdad comes from the Bible, which mentions the town of Ashdod—though the station was called Ashdod, the "o" in the name was rounded into an "a" through use. Eventually, the spelling caught up, and Ashdod became Ashdad. The name inspired the silly story about the young boy making potash—he remarked to his father, "Goodness, we've plenty of <u>ash</u>, <u>dad</u>."

BALMER'S ISLAND. This community in McNab Township is now called Stewartville, but from 1865 to 1872 the local post office was known as either Bulmer's Island or Balmer's Island. The origin of the name is told in an old logging story, of which there are several contradictory versions. In the early 19th century, a log driver named Bulmer (or Balmer) was guiding a raft of timber down the Madawaska when his raft wrecked on an island. In one version of the story, Bulmer was drowned—another version says he was stranded on the island until his fellow log drivers could rescue him. To remember the event, the local post office later opened under Bulmer's name.

BISSETT CREEK. Bissett Creek hamlet on Highway 17 is in the isolated northern Township of Head, Clara, & Maria. The hamlet is one of the smallest addresses left in Southern Ontario, with (at last count) seven families receiving their mail at Bissett Creek. The creek that flows through town was named sometime in the 1840s or 1850s for an early settler in the area—his story seems to have been lost, even though his name was preserved on this tiny village.

BLACK DONALD LAKE. This artificial lake was created on the boundary between Renfrew and Frontenac Counties in the late 1960s. The lake flooded the old mining village of Black Donald, where a huge deposit of graphite had been worked for several decades. The name of Black Donald evokes the Scottish character of southeastern Renfrew, and one of two Scotsmen may have given their name to the community: "Black Donald" Macdonald was an early log driver on the Madawaska, and "Black Donald" Kennelly owned the land on which the Black Donald mines operated. A post office opened here in 1896 under the name Black Donald, so Macdonald may be the Black Donald the postmaster had in mind. It was not until 1944 that the presence of the mines was recognized by a name change to Black Donald Mines.

BULLIES ACRE. "Bullies Acre" has long been applied to a spot near Kerr Line in the Township of Ross. You can't find Bullies Acre on the maps, but local residents still remember the story behind the name. Sometime in the 19th century, the people of Ross decided to build themselves a new church. To build it, they hired some laborers from outside the township—in some versions of the story, they were French Canadians from across the nearby Ottawa River. When the church was nearly complete, the local people decided to hold a service there. However, the laborers, after liberal helpings of whiskey, started to harass the church-goers. The outraged citizens drove off the drunken workers and finished the church themselves. Ever since, this spot has been called Bullies Acre. There's also a possibility the name may have been handed down from the Irish, as an old graveyard in Dublin is known as Bullies Acre. The name is a corruption of the Gaelic word *baile*, "town" (i.e., "the town's acre.")

CHENAUX. The tiny hamlet of Chenaux (pronounced "shen-O") is near the Ontario-Québec border in Ross Township. The hamlet is often referred to as simply the Four Corners because of its size. The French word *chenaux* means "the channels," referring to the nearby Ottawa River—the Ottawa splits into two arms around a small island near Chenaux's location. The community, which survives on cross-border traffic, did not receive its first post office until 1953. The office was closed during the postal service cuts of the late '60s.

CORMAC. "Cormac" looks odd because Cormac is actually missing the first part of its name. In September, 1895, a post office called MacCormac opened in Sebastapol Township. (Father James MacCormac had founded the local church parish.) But the government quickly discovered they had already approved a MacCormac P.O. somewhere else in Canada. To solve the problem, the "Mac" was dropped from this community's name, leaving just "Cormac." Cormac P.O. is still open almost one hundred years later.

DACRE. Dacre village is best known as the home of Magnetic Hill, where (thanks to an optical illusion) cars seem to roll uphill. The hamlet, located on the Opeongo Line, has been called Dacre since the post office opened there in 1865. (The office only recently shut down.) The name may have been given because of a connection between an English stream and Lord Brougham, for whom the township surrounding our Dacre was named. Brougham's land holdings may have included the watershed of the Dacre, a sluggish little brook in Cumbria. There is also a village known as Dacre on the banks of this brook. The name comes from a hazily identified word in ancient British, probably meaning "to trickle." Dacre is pronounced like the word "acre" ("DAY-kur.")

DEUX-RIVIÈRES. Isolated in the spectacular hills of Clara Township, tiny Deux-Rivières may have the most arresting location of any community in Eastern Ontario. The hamlet's name seems relatively straight forward—it means "two rivers" in French—but the question of which two rivers is a little confusing. Deux-Rivières village is right at the junction of Deux-Rivières Creek and the Ottawa River, but apparently these are not the "two rivers" intended by the name. Opposite town, on the Québec side of the Ottawa, another river called the Maganassippi also empties into the Ottawa. This is the pair of rivers the postmaster had in mind when Deux-Rivières was named in 1866, and may also account for the community's name being French. Unusually, Canada Post has allowed both the hyphen and appropriate accent to be used for this name. (See Chute à Blondeau under Prescott County for details about this practice in Ontario.)

EEYORE LAKE. However unlikely it may seem, this lake really is named for the character Eeyore in A. A. Milne's *Winnie the Pooh!* In 1947, a superintendent at Algonquin Provincial Park decided to name several anonymous lakes in Maria Township after Milne's creations. The move was approved, and today we have Eeyore Lake, Christopher Robin Lake, Tigger Lake, Pooh Lake, Roo Lake, Kanga Lake, Owl Lake, and Piglet Lake. All are in an inaccessible part of central Maria.

FOYMOUNT. Foymount hamlet is the highest point in Eastern Ontario, perched on a mountain overlooking the beautiful scenery of Sebastapol Township. Because of its location, Foymount was chosen as the site for a radar station —the base was designed to detect Russian planes or missiles travelling over the north pole. A subdivision was built to house the officers working at the base, and these houses still form the bulk of the village today. Fortunately, the radar station (part of what was called the Pinetree Line) has now been dismantled, and Foymount has returned to the peaceful place it was before the Cold War started. The name Foymount was invented by the first postmaster, John Foy, who ran the office from his hotel.

JEFFREYS LAKE. This small, elongated lake is on the east side of Cobden village, though you'll get an argument as to whether it's called Jeffreys Lake or not. As I'm told, Jeffreys Lake is referred to as Jeffreys Lake, Olmstead Lake, or Logan Lake, depending on whether one is a Jeffrey, an Olmstead, or a Logan! Jeffreys seems to be the approved choice now, but I've seen "Olmstead Lake" on at least one map . . . the argument continues.

KAMANISKEG LAKE. See Hastings County.

KASZUBY. The hamlet of Kaszuby (pronounced "ka-SHOO-bee") is in Radcliffe Township, a short distance southeast of Barrys Bay. Even though the community didn't get a summer post office until 1961, the name has been around since the 1800s. When German and Polish settlers came to Renfrew County around the mid-19th century, they were accompanied by a small party of Kaszubs. The Kaszubs were (and still are) a Slavic-speaking minority in Poland, and offers of new land drew them overseas from their crowded home country. These Kaszub settlers traveled up the Opeongo Line and—having asked for their own settlement separate from the Poles—homesteaded near Wadsworth Lake. A few kilometres away, the Poles founded their own village of Wilno (see below). Unfortunately, Kaszuby P.O. was one of the first offices closed in the latest round of postal service cuts.

KHARTUM. This tiny hamlet is on Highway 41 in Griffith Township. The name (pronounced "car-TOOM") definitely comes from Africa, but the spelling might throw you off the actual source—Khartoum is the capital city of the Sudan. The name, approved for a post office here in 1908, was inspired by the exploits of several Renfrew County men. In the 1880s, several Valley residents had served on a British military expedition to Egypt and the Sudan. Khartoum was almost certainly one of the places they would have seen on that tour of duty.

LA PASSE. La Passe (often said "la pawss" in the Valley) is a hamlet in Westmeath Township, just opposite the northwestern tip of Grand Calumet Island. The community was called Gower Point until 1906, when the post office there was renamed "La Passe." The traditional source ascribed to La Passe, which means "the passing" in French, is the yearly migration of Canada geese up the Ottawa Valley. The Valley is one of the major bird migration routes in North America.

MOOR LAKE STATION. This isolated hamlet was once the home of a post office and a railway station in northwestern Rolph Township. The lake of the name is a short ways up the Canadian Pacific line—a family named Moor settled in the vicinity in the 19th century. Moor Lake Station P.O. closed in 1963, after which residents had to travel the bush road to Rolphton for their mail. There are only one or two houses left at the old station site today.

THE NEWFOUNDOUT. This oddly named hamlet has almost disappeared into the forests of Grattan Township. The Newfoundout was along the 7th Line of Grattan, several kilometres west of the crucial Opeongo Settlement Road. The name of the Newfoundout (which is usually "the Newfoundout," not just "Newfoundout") was probably given to describe the hamlet—a recent settlement, newly "found out" by Renfrew's early settlers. Fortunately, the name of the Newfoundout is still remembered in the Valley, even though the community is almost history.

OPEONGO. See Nipissing District.

OSCEOLA. A hamlet in Bromley Township goes by the name Osceola (pronounced "AWS-ee-oh-luh.") Osceola has no connection to Bromley, Renfrew County, or even directly to Canada—a chief of the Seminole First Nation, which rebelled against American aggression in the 1830s, was called Osceola. The name was approved for a post office in Bromley in 1863, and might have come from the same American name list as Little Britain (see Victoria County). Osceola is just west of Cobden.

PAUGH LAKE. Paugh (pronounced "PAW") Lake is the name of both a lake in Burns Township and a hamlet in Sherwood Township. The lake was named first, a local post office also opening as Paugh Lake in 1912. According to Alan Rayburn in his study of Renfrew County place names, Paugh is derived from the Algonquin expression *paquiac sagagan*, meaning "the shallow lake."

QUADEVILLE. This eye-catching name (pronounced as it's written, "QUAD-ville") has been used for a Lyndoch Township hamlet since the turn of the century. Originally, the community was given the fairly pedestrian name of "Strathtay" by the government. Local residents objected to this imposition and demanded the post office be called "Quadville." The Quade family were some of the first settlers in the area, and today a good half-dozen Quades can be found in the phone book. The change from Strathtay to "Quadville" was made in 1907, and in 1921 the name was adjusted to include the "e." Quadeville now claims to have been a hide-out for infamous American gangster Al Capone!

ROCHER FENDU. "Russia Fundy," as folks in the Valley say, is a hamlet on the Ottawa River opposite Grand Calumet Island. The phrase "rocher fendu" means "split rock" in French, and describes a nearby channel on the river. A widening of the river near Kerr Line is also called "Lac du Rocher-Fendu." Rocher Fendu is one of several French names found along this section of the Ottawa (for example, see also "La Passe," above).

SCHUTT. See Zadow.

SHADY NOOK. This charming name was used for a small rural post office in Stafford Township. The name was apparently given to describe the quiet, leafy setting of the hamlet, which was a postal village from 1895 to 1914.

SIMPSON'S PIT. This odd (and somewhat uninspiring!) name was given to a post office in Hagarty Township, near Killaloe. From 1913 to 1925, the office operated at a mine site—owned by the Simpson family—in Hagarty's 6th Concession. The mine had its own flag stop on the now-defunct Booth railway line into Algonquin. Though the mine is history, you can occasionally find the site marked as just "Simpsons" on detailed maps of the Valley.

STONECLIFFE. The name of Stonecliffe village is not particularly remarkable. However, there's a story in the bewildering series of name changes that finally arrived at "Stonecliffe." In 1870, this remote village in Head Township was established as "Rockcliffe," after the village which is now a ritzy suburb of

Ottawa. The post office department quickly decided that there was too much potential for misdirected mail between the two Rockcliffes, so in 1909 the name was altered to "Stonecliff." Subsequent to that, the government found it had already granted a "Stonecliff P.O.," so an "e" was added to distinguish the two. The CPR avoided the whole question by naming its railway stop there "Stone Station." Stonecliffe is now the municipal seat for Head, Clara, and Maria Township.

TATTY HILL. In the slang of the Valley Irish, a "tatty" is a potato, and I'll bet at one time you could find potatoes planted on this hill near Barryvale! The area is very sparsely populated, and not amenable to farming, so potatoes may be in short supply on Tatty Hill today.

WABA. Waba is the Ojibwa word for "white," and a number of locations in southeastern Renfrew have used it as a place name. There is a hamlet called Waba in McNab Township, situated on the banks of Waba Creek. Nearby, the name has been translated into English in White Lake and White Lake Post Office, which has been open since 1848. Waba village was a postal hamlet from 1889 to 1948. The word is pronounced "WAH-buh."

WILNO. "Canada's first Polish settlement," as it bills itself, Wilno village in Hagarty Township is the heart of Renfrew's Polish community. The village is an attractive place, dominated by the enormous church on Highway 60. Wilno was founded during the 1860s, when a small group of settlers crossed over to Canada from Wilno, Poland. (The original Wilno is now part of Belarus.) The name was approved in 1885, and today a special postmark illustrates Wilno's Polish heritage.

WOERMKE. See Zadow.

WOITO. See Zadow.

WOLFE RAPIDS. A small falls near Wolfe Post Office in Lyndoch Township was dubbed "Wolfe Rapids." The office was definitely named for the first postmaster, John Wolfe—however, there is an old tale that the rapids were named because wolves would dig up and eat the corpses of drowned log drivers from the foot of the falls!

ZADOW. This old post office name from South Algona Township is one of several named after German postmasters. It was common practice in the 19th century to name offices after the first postmaster, and the presence of so many German settlers in central Renfrew resulted in distinctive office names. Zadow (pronounced "ZAY-dough") was named for the Zadows, of which there were three related families in South Algona. Other offices in this category include: *Woito* (pronounced "WOY-toe") in Alice; *Woermke* ("WORM-key") in Sebastapol, there being two Woermke families there around the turn of the century; and *Schutt* (in Raglan, pronounced "SHUT") for postmaster Christie Schutt. The surnames Woito and Zadow are actually Wendish, the Wends being the German-speaking people of the German-Polish border area. These post offices have since closed, though all four names—Schutt in particular—are known around the Valley.

11. Frontenac County

Frontenac is the only Eastern Ontario county with a French name. In 1673, the French explorer La Salle established a fort at the mouth of the Cataraqui. He called the new settlement "Fort Frontenac" for the then-governor of New France, the Comte de Frontenac. The fort was eventually destroyed, but the name was so prominent that the English still knew it when this county was named 125-plus years later. (A county in southeastern Québec is also known as Frontenac after the same governor.) The place names of Ontario's Frontenac are mostly English in the south, given by the English Loyalists who first settled the county. But in the northern part of Frontenac, the names are far more unusual—aboriginal, European, and American place-names are jumbled together in an highly unlikely mix. It is here, between the Mississippi and the Madawaska Rivers, that you'll find some of the most distinctive place names in Ontario.

ARDEN. The village of Arden is just south of Highway 7 in Kennebec Township. Arden was born in the lumbering days of the mid-1800s, when the timber around Big Clear Lake drew several sawmills to the area. The community was first called "Clear Valley" after the lake, but when a post office was granted the government insisted on a new name—there was already a Clear Valley P.O. somewhere else. The postmaster eventually came up with the suggestion Arden, from the poem "Enoch Arden" by Alfred, Lord Tennyson. In the poem, Enoch Arden is a long-suffering sailor who's given up for dead by his fiancee. He returns to find her married to someone else, but decides not to contact her and destroy her new life. Arden is an uncommon English surname, probably tracing its roots to the Warwickshire village of Arden. In ancient British (the forerunner of modern Welsh), Arden means "a steep place," which is not a bad description of the hilly country around our Arden.

ARDOCH. This peaceful hamlet is on the Mississippi River in Clarendon Township, just east of Highway 506. Like most of its neighbors, Ardoch was a lumber town, and in the early 1900s claimed to have the largest sawmill in the whole of North America. The name "Ardoch" can be traced back to Scotland, where there is a village called Ardoch in Tayside. This Ardoch was the home of the Stevensons, one of the first European families to reach Clarendon Township. The Stevensons would have met many Algonquin people during their time in Ardoch, and Clarendon Township still has a large Algonquin population known as "the Ardoch Algonquin First Nation." As in the word loch, the "ch" in Ardoch is pronounced like a "k" (i.e. "AHR-dawk.")

BALLYNAHINCH. The tongue-twisting Ballynahinch (pronounced bal-EE-nuh-hinch) is the former name of Glenvale hamlet in Kingston Township. The village post office opened as Ballynahinch in 1858, but because of the confusing spelling and pronunciation (to non-Irish people, obviously!) the office was renamed "Glenvale" in 1863. The Kick & Push Railway station near the village also went by "Glenvale." The original Loyalist population of Kingston township was supplemented by later Irish immigrants, and Ballynahinch was one of the hamlets to which these new settlers gravitated. In Irish Gaelic, Ballynahinch (*Baile na hInse*) means "the homestead of the island," referring to the island of Ireland itself. The name occurs several times around Ireland, most prominently on a town in County Down. "Ballynahinch" is no longer heard in Kingston Township.

BELLROCK. Bellrock is a substantial little mill town in Portland Township, just off Frontenac County Road 7. The community boomed early in its history because of its perfect location—huge amounts of timber in the Depot Lakes system were floated down Depot Creek to the sawmill at Bellrock, providing steady work (and spin-off jobs for small businesses) well into this century. The community's name was coined in the mid-19th century: Bell was the name of the local mill-owner, and the village was located in the rocky shield country of the Frontenac Axis. Thus, "Bell-rock." The name was approved for the local post office in 1861 and remains well known throughout Frontenac County. County Road 7 is referred to as "the Bellrock Road" by local residents.

BELLYBUTTON CENTRE & CROTCH LAKE. These two places can be found in Frontenac's Palmerston Township, which can lay claim to many of the county's most unusual place-names. Bellybutton Centre (and I'm not making this up!) was the name given to a crossroads on the Ardoch Road by local sawmill workers. So far as we know, no logger had it in mind to immortalize this particular part of his anatomy. The name was really given because the crossroads was located just above (wait for it . . .) CROTCH LAKE. People from away are often taken aback to find cottage properties for sale at a place called Crotch Lake, but there's a perfectly good (non-anatomical!) reason for the name. The lake has an extremely sharp bend in the middle, creating two distinct arms . . . or legs, maybe. This kind of angle between a tree trunk and a branch is called a crotch, and so the shape of the lake inspired the name "Crotch Lake."

BREWERS MILLS. If temperance crusader Letitia Youmans had ever got wind of this name from Pittsburgh Township, you can almost picture her, mallet in hand, at the hotel door! So far as we know, no brewing ever happened at Brewers Mills—one John Brewer owned two mills here in the early 1800s. When the Rideau Canal was built, both his mills had to be dynamited to make way for the construction. (The buildings stood where Upper and Lower Brewers Locks are today.) After Brewer died, local residents decided to honor him by naming their post office "Brewers Mills" in 1852. The office closed in 1970 and, until the addition of a recent subdivision, the community had dwindled to a few older homes on Highway 15.

BUCKSHOT / PLEVNA. One hundred and twenty years ago, the residents of Buckshot almost resorted to using their namesake on one another over the name "Buckshot." This Clarendon Township village, which grew up around a mill in the mid-1800s, called itself Buckshot after a local Algonquin or Cree family. Two of the Buckshots, Zebediah and Muchawan, are recorded as having worked as log drivers on the nearby Madawaska River. The European settlers depended heavily on the Algonquins to survive, and the people of northern Clarendon honored their aboriginal neighbors by naming the local post office "Buckshot" in 1872.

However, a heavily starched bureaucrat in the Post Office Department decided Buckshot was not a sufficiently dignified name for the new community. Therefore, Buckshot had to go. In the fall of 1877, local residents met to pick a new name, but the discussion quickly turned into an argument. No decision was made at the first meeting, and over the next few weeks the people of Buckshot got increasingly hostile with one another about what to call their village. Finally, one local farmer broke the log-jam by suggesting "Plevna." Plevna Pass (now called Pleven Pass) was a strategic mountain road in Bulgaria—great battles had been fought there as far back as the time of Alexander the Great. The acrimony in town probably inspired the farmer's choice! The people of Buckshot agreed with his proposal, and on 01 November 1877, the post office was renamed "Plevna P.O." The office is still operating today in Miller's General Store. The name Buckshot has survived on Buckshot Creek in town and on a nearby lake.

BUZZTOWN (VERONA). The Portland Township village of Verona has gone under several names since its founding in the early 1800s. One part of the town was first called "Richardson," and the town's railway station was first located there. At the same time, the southern half of the village became known as "Buzztown," a name that is no longer used but is warmly remembered in the area. There are two possible explanations for Buzztown: one story says the name was coined because the main street was so busy it was "buzzing," while the other story says the "buzz" in Buzztown was the village's sawmill. Both Buzztown and Richardson were displaced by "Verona" (the name of an Italian city, suggested by the local hotel proprietors, who were Italian) in 1858.

CANONTO. The Townships of North Canonto and South Canonto are at the northeastern corner of Frontenac County. The townships are sparsely settled, with only one hamlet in South Canonto and none at all in North Canonto. The name of the townships is a real puzzler: our only clue is a strange passage from Herbert Gardiner's *Nothing But Names* (1899). Gardiner's exact words are that "an aged Indian told a Kingston gentleman that Canonto was the name of a Frenchman who lived there many years ago." Maybe this "Kingston gentleman" was Gardiner's only source for the story—why else was this information relevant? It's a bit of a mystery. There's no trace of this Canonto, and the name wasn't given to the townships until at least 1858, by which time French rule had been over for almost a century in Eastern Ontario. To date, this is all we know about the name of North and South Canonto.

CATARAQUI. Cataraqui is one of the oldest place-names still in use in Eastern Ontario—though they might not recognize the spelling, French fur traders of the 17th century would know the exact location of Cataraqui. The name is properly pronounced "cat-a-ROCK-way," which invariably throws people from outside the Kingston area. The modern spelling, one of fifty-odd spellings of this name, is a corruption of an Algonquin or Iroquois word. Several linguists and historians have made a stab at identifying that word, but we really don't know what was meant by "Cataraqui." One linguist linked it to an expression meaning "bounteous land," with an ending (-kooi) used only by aboriginal people in the vicinity of Lake Ontario. However, the name Cataraqui has been used and abused for so long we will probably never be able to identify it conclusively. It is a unique and attractive name regardless of what it means.

CROTCH LAKE. See Bellybutton Centre.

DEERDOCH. Deerdoch P.O. was located in the home of an Oso Township settler during the 1870s and 1880s. The name is virtually unknown in Oso today, and is recorded in only a few surviving documents from the immediate post-Confederation period. One story tells of how the postmaster was set upon by a gang of thieves as he was bringing the mail back from the railway station. Calmly, he pulled out a long knife, and as one of the thieves was climbing onto his wagon, stabbed the attacker right through the hand. (The Royal Mail meant business in those days!) The name "Deerdoch" was probably coined just for the office—the nearby village of Ardoch plus the good deer-hunting in North Frontenac may have been the inspiration.

FERMOY. The one-time mining town of Fermoy is on Frontenac Road 8 in Bedford Township. The early settlement of the area is not well recorded, but it is known the land was promised to the Algonquin First Nation as a reserve. The government later reneged on its promise of a reserve, and instead the land was opened up to European settlement. Fermoy Post Office opened to serve these new settlers in November of 1854. The name—which is pronounced with the emphasis on the last syllable, i.e., fur-MOY—comes from a town in County Cork. The community, noted for its ancient monastery, is called *Fhear Maí,* meaning "the men of the plain." Our Fermoy has been quiet since the mines closed down just before World War II.

FERNLEIGH. The village of Fernleigh in Clarendon Township long prospered on tourism—the village is one of the few access points to beautiful Kash-wakamak Lake. Unfortunately, the little Fernleigh Post Office shut down in 1980 when the general store went out of business. Traditionally, the name "Fernleigh" was said to have been given by a local schoolboy. Back in 1902, the teacher at the Fernleigh school asked her students to come up with a name for their new post office. One boy looked out the window and noticed a large carpet of ferns on the marshy soil. He put up his hand and immediately suggested "Fernleigh." The name was later approved by the community.

HARLOWE. Harlowe village is a short distance east of Highway 41 in Barrie Township. The village was born as a logging settlement, and logging continues there on a smaller scale today. Harlowe is remembered as the home of Mrs. Clifford, the mysterious "Herb Woman of Harlowe." Before the turn of the century, her herbal cures were often the only medical attention available. The original Harlow (the "e" is a Canadian addition) can be found in Essex, England. The name means "the army mound" in Old English, and the village was designated as the meeting place for what is still called "The Hundred of Harlow." For centuries, England has been divided into units called hundreds, which are something like little municipal councils. At one time, each Hundred was required to provide so many able-bodied men to fight when the king demanded. Thus, the point where the militia met in this particular hundred in Essex became known as "the army mound," Harlow. The name was designated for our village's post office in 1871, and (with one hiatus) Harlowe P.O. was open until 1969.

HARROWSMITH / SPIKE'S CORNERS. One of the most distinctive place names in Eastern Ontario is Harrowsmith, made famous by *Harrowsmith Magazine*. The rural issues magazine was published in nearby Camden East until new owners moved the offices to Metro Toronto. Harrowsmith has been on the map in Portland Township since 1857—earlier, the community had been called Spike's Corners for settler Brian Spike. He had opened the village's first general store and simultaneously ran the post office starting in 1849. The origin of the name "Harrowsmith" is not certain, but the generally accepted story is that Harrowsmith is a play on the name of Harry Smith. Sir Harry Smith was a powerful lumber baron in Frontenac County and, briefly, the area's member of provincial parliament. Smith had a hand in naming many communities in south Frontenac, so it's not surprising the people eventually decided to name a post office after him.

HERCHMER'S NOSE. This entertaining name was given to what's now called Lemoine's Point in Kingston Township. The point, now protected in a conservation area, was originally the farm of a Loyalist settler named Herchmer. Because of the rounded shape of the point, it was therefore dubbed Herchmer's Nose! The name hasn't been heard in the Township for a very long time, Lemoine's (for a French land-owner, Jean Le Moyne) being the only modern name.

KENNEBEC. Created in 1823, the Township of Kennebec is in northern Frontenac. A large part of Kennebec's population lives in Arden (see above) or in the hamlet of Henderson. The township took its name from the aboriginal languages of Maine—the word "kennebec" means "winding" or "serpentine," usually in reference to a river or lake. The choice of Kennebec for this township may have been inspired by Kennebec Lake, which is a long, narrow, winding body of water.

The name Kennebec is used several times in the New England states, most prominently for a river in Maine (which matches the serpentine image) and for what was called the "Kennebeck Road." In the 1820s, this road was constructed from Boston through to Québec to facilitate trade between Boston and Montréal. This brought the name "Kennebec" into regular use in Québec—today, one of Québec's Senatorial divisions is still called Kennebec. The word Kennebec can also be found in Longfellow's famous poem "Hiawatha," in which he describes ". . . the Kennebeek [sic], the great serpents/Coiling, playing in the water."

LAKE OPINICON. This beautiful lake is part of the Rideau watershed, running from the northern edge of Storrington Township through to the village of Chaffeys Locks (see Leeds County). The community called Lake Opinicon is down a long and treacherous side-road from Perth Road Village. The village grew rapidly on the strength of the lumber industry and a nearby phosphate mine. A postmaster was appointed in 1871, and the office took the aboriginal name "Opinicon," meaning "narrows" in the Mississauga language. (The word is usually pronounced "oh-PIN-uh-cawn.") The village became a virtual ghost town after the mines closed. There is now a sizable cottage community here.

LANTANA. From 1912 to 1919, Lantana Post Office operated near the intersection of the Lavant Station side-road and what's now Highway 509. The name is still remembered in Palmerston Township, but no one seems to remember the source. There is a Lantana in Florida, which may have appeared on the American place-name list of the post office department (see Little Britain under Victoria County). With the huge number of post offices opened just after the turn of the century, the government was probably looking *very* far afield for office names, possibly even as far as rural Florida. One source indicated the name "Lantana" was inspired by the Latin name of a flower, though this flower hasn't presented itself yet.

MISSISSAGAGON LAKE. Mississagagon Lake is right at the centre of Barrie Township. Barrie is criss-crossed by several large lakes like Mississagagon, and there's almost more water than land in the township. Frequently, the name Mississagagon (pronounced "miss-us-SAG-uh-gawn") has been given the meaning "the great headwaters"—the word was said to come from the same root as the more famous Mississippi River. However, the Algonquin people of north Frontenac have now identified the real meaning of "Mississagagon" as "a place (or something) that you would notice." Obviously, some feature of this large, attractive lake—perhaps just its natural setting—inspired the Algonquins to remember it as a place that you would notice.

MOSQUE LAKE. This small lake on the Clarendon-Miller border has had a deceptive name change. Originally the lake was called "Mosquito," but to avoid confusion with the dozens of other Mosquito Lakes in Ontario, someone abbreviated the name to just "Mosque." The inspiration for this odd change is a mystery—there isn't a mosque anywhere near the area, nor is the lake shaped in any way that might suggest the name "Mosque." The Snow Colonization Road once ran just north of Mosque Lake.

MYERS CAVE. The hamlet of Myers Cave takes its name from one of Eastern Ontario's most enduring legends. Long before active settlement came to Barrie Township, a frontiersman named Myer (or Meyer) lived here with the First Nations people. One day, one of the aboriginal men promised to show Myer a fabulous silver cave—as the story goes, the silver hung like icicles from the ceiling. However, Myer had to agree to be blindfolded going to and coming from the cave. With visions of becoming an instant millionaire, Myer agreed. He was led to the cave, which was exactly as advertised. The silver was everywhere, beyond reckoning. Myer was then taken back to his cabin. Desperately the woodsman tried to figure out the path to the cave. The search went on and on and on, for many years, until finally Myer went mad from trying to find the silver cave. Ever since, people have been searching for Myers Cave. There are caves in Barrie Township, formed by underground rivers during the Ice Age, but so far no one has discovered the cave of silver. This story is so well known and so strongly attached to this location that in the 1890s the post office was named Myers Cave. The little village only has about twenty people today.

OCONTO. Oconto was established as a station on the Kick & Push Railway, just south of St. George's Lake. The word "Oconto" is from the Dakotah people of Wisconsin, and means (depending on who you ask) "the red river" or "where there are pickerel." It's not clear how the name traveled all the way from Wisconsin to Oso Township, but it's likely one of the K & P's American backers knew the original Oconto. (See "Lithia Station" and "Pana Station" under Russell County for other instances of migrating American place-names.) Another possible link is that the Holt Timber Company—which worked major areas of northeastern Ontario—had its headquarters in Oconto, Wisconsin. It's not clear if Holt owned any land in North Frontenac, but it's possible.

Close to the station, a children's summer camp on Eagle Lake also adopted the name Oconto. Camp Oconto was a busy spot during the summer, the camp operating from the 1920s on into the late 1960s. A summer post office called "Camp Oconto" was located at Eagle Lake until about 1970. The name Oconto is usually pronounced "oh-CAWN-toe."

OMPAH. This odd place name from Palmerston Township is pronounced "AWM-pah," not "OOM-pah." While the village is famous for its Ompah Stomp music festival, polka music is definitely not a part of the program! (Remember, "Ompah" rhymes with "Stomp.")The village's location on Palmerston Lake gave rise to its name. The First Nations People of North Frontenac knew this place as the "long crossing" or "long portage" (ompah)—a lengthy portage was needed to reach Palmerston Lake from the much-travelled Mississippi River, several kilometres to the south. The village itself has been called Ompah since 1865.

ORE CHIMNEY & THE STAR OF THE EAST. The Ore Chimney mine was a failed gold-mining venture during the short-lived Hastings Gold Rush. The mine was in the rugged bush of Barrie Township, between Cloyne and Myers Cave (see above). The name Ore Chimney is simply descriptive—however, one investor in the disastrous mine (not a single ounce of gold came out of Ore Chimney) said it was called Ore Chimney because "that's where gold went up in smoke!" Another, more successful gold-mine in Barrie was called The Star of the East. Some kind of Biblical connotation may have been meant (a miraculously successful gold-mine?!), but it's impossible to know for sure. A few scattered remains of the mines still exist, but the names see no modern use in Barrie.

OSO. One of the smallest, but most populous, townships in North Frontenac, Oso (pronounced "OH-so") also has one of the most unusual township names in Eastern Ontario. The word "oso" means "bear" in Spanish, and the decision to apply the name here was made by Canadian governor Sir Peregrine Maitland. Maitland, who was governor during the 1810s, had served a tour of duty with the Duke of Wellington in Spain. To commemorate this tour, Maitland decided to give several Eastern Ontario townships Spanish names. One of the first so named was Oso—the others include Mariposa ("butterfly") in Victoria, Mono ("monkey") in Dufferin County, and Zorra ("vixen") in Oxford County. In 1878, a railway station on the Kick & Push was also named "Oso" from its location in the township.

Over the years, at least two other stories have grown up about the name Oso. One says the letters O-S-O meant "our soldiers overseas," a story that was probably started during the First World War and passed down to today. The other story says the phrase "Oh-So" was used at milking time to calm the cow. Neither story is true, but they show how much oral tradition has built up around Eastern Ontario's place-names.

OSSA. Ossa Post Office was located somewhere in southeastern Olden Township, probably near Long Lake. The name Ossa looks suspiciously like Oso, though they have no connection—Mount Ossa is really a mountain in central Greece. A Greek myth says the Titans, a race of powerful giants, tried to invade the Greek gods' mountain stronghold of Olympus by piling Mount Ossa upon another, smaller mountain. With the two mountains stacked one atop the other, the Titans were able to reach Olympus, but were defeated by Zeus and the other gods. The choice of Ossa was made by the first postmaster, James Sanderson, in 1883.

The name Ossa didn't last long, though, because there was almost certain confusion between Ossa P.O. and Oso Station (frequently shortened to just Oso) P.O. The government figured Sanderson meant "Osso" instead of "Ossa," and issued the first postmark hammers with that spelling. Sanderson eventually got the spelling corrected, but the confusion undoubtedly persisted. Ossa P.O. was eventually closed in 1892.

PLEVNA. See Buckshot.

SEOULS CORNERS. This hamlet in central Olden Township is listed as having an official population of three! There are no corners at the Corners today, but at one time the hamlet was at the intersection of the Bell Line Road and the north-south Frontenac Settlement Road. (For about ten kilometers, the Frontenac Road has totally disappeared between Highway 7 and Coxvale.) The name "Seouls" looks like it might have had something to do with South Korea, but the Seouls intended here were the local Soles family. How or why the spelling was changed from "Soles" to "Seouls" seems to have been forgotten.

SHARBOT LAKE. The largest community in North Frontenac, Sharbot Lake is at the busy intersection of Highways 38 and 7. The village, which is the municipal seat of Oso Township, is on a narrow isthmus separating the two halves of Sharbot's namesake lake. Until the 1960s, the community was also at the junction of two railroads, the east-west Lakeshore Line and the north-south Kick & Push line. While the tracks have been lifted, there are still many residents who remember the peak of the railroad era. The name "Sharbot" comes from the aboriginal Sharbot family—a photographic portrait of the Sharbots now hangs in the community hall. The Sharbots were one of many aboriginal families who travelled from the Deux-Montagnes area, just north of Montréal, into this region to hunt and trap. The Sharbots were not the only native family here, but in the 1820s they were one of the first contacted by the advancing European settlers. The lake was first called Crooked Lake from its irregular shape, but "Sharbot" was substituted soon afterwards. The post office opened as Sharbot Lake in 1878.

SNOW ROAD STATION. This one-time railway village in Palmerston Township sounds as if it's socked away in the trackless north. In fact, the village's name has nothing to do with the weather—John A. Snow was the surveyor of the local township, and of the old Snow (or Mississippi) Settlement Road. The Snow Road ran, right across north Frontenac and Lennox & Addington and into Hastings, ending near L'Amable (see Hastings County). When the Kick & Push Railway crossed that road, "Snow Road Station" came into being. The village was originally two distinct settlements, one called Snow Road, the other known as McLaren's Depot (for lumber baron Peter McLaren). The two were amalgamated under a single post office in 1914. After a brief hiatus in the mid-'80s, Snow Road Station P.O. is now back in business.

SPIKE'S CORNERS. See Harrowsmith.

STAR OF THE EAST. See Ore Chimney.

TICHBORNE. A native of the original Tichborne, in Hampshire, England, suggested this name for a village near Hinchinbrooke Township's eastern boundary. (Until 1874, the village had been called Parham Junction, as this was the Kick & Push Railway station nearest Parham village. Parham is about two kilometers west of Tichborne.) The English Tichborne has a remarkable story to its name. The Tichbornes were an ancient noble family who, around a.d. 1150, began an annual distribution of flour to the poor. Lady Tichborne, who started the practice, decreed it must continue forever and laid a curse on any of her descendants who defied her wishes. Remarkably, the annual distribution lasted until 1795, when one of the Tichbornes gave it up. Within a few years, the Tichborne family was stricken with illness and a series of financial disasters. When another family member resumed the tradition in 1835, the family's luck took a permanent turn for the better. In Old English, "Ticcaburna" meant "the young goats' stream."

UNGAVA. During the days of the Lakeshore Line railway, there was a siding between Sharbot Lake and Maberly called Ungava. The name's source is no mystery—Ungava Bay is at the northern tip of Québec. The word "ungava," meaning "far away, distant land," is from the language of the Québec Inuit. There doesn't seem to be any written record as to why this siding was called Ungava. The siding's location is now inaccessible, though the name is still known in the Sharbot Lake area.

ZANESVILLE. In the 1880s and 1890s, the Zanesville iron mine was an important economic player in Bedford Township. The mine was located on Thirteen Island Lake, just south of Glendower hamlet and near the Kick & Push Railway line. So much iron ore went out of Zanesville to the nearby station at Godfrey that Godfrey was often called "Iron Ore Junction." The name "Zanesville" was taken from a town in the American Mid-west, where the mine owners probably had their base of operations. Our Zanesville had a post office from 1886 until 1893, and once the mine closed, the name "Zanesville" disappeared from the map.

12. Lennox & Addington County

The County of Lennox & Addington contains the oldest Loyalist settlement in Ontario, Adolphustown, and was the boyhood home of Sir John A. Macdonald. John Graves Simcoe, the governor who established the boundaries of most Eastern Ontario counties, intended Lennox & Addington to be two separate entities. Eventually, the plan was abandoned in 1864 because population growth was (and is) so slow in the area. The county retained its dual name anyway—it is the only single county in Ontario to have two names. The Lennox of Lennox & Addington was Charles Lennox, Duke of Richmond, a radical democratic reformer of the 18th century. His nephew was later Canada's governor-general. The Scottish surname of the Lennoxes means "the place of many elms" in Gaelic. The Addington in question is Henry Addington, Viscount Sidmouth, prime minister of Great Britain from 1801 to 1804.

ABINGER. The Township of Abinger is in the northern part of Lennox & Addington, and encompasses the hamlet of Vennachar (*see below*). The name, which is pronounced "AH-bin-jur," comes from another English politician: the dramatically named Sir James Scarlett, Baron Abinger, was a senior cabinet minister in the early 1800s. He and Henry Addington would have been acquainted, which accounts for Abinger's name on this township. His title came from the Surrey village of Abinger, south of London. Literally translated from Old English, Abinger is "the enclosure of Abba."

BALAHECK. The hamlet of Balaheck, in Sheffield Township, has one of the most confused stories of any Eastern Ontario place-name. Even answering the question "Where the heck *is* Balaheck?" is a problem, because Balaheck's exact limits depend on who you ask. A road northeast out of town is known locally as the Balaheck Road, though there's no sign to indicate this is the name.

No matter where Balaheck is, the community was first known as Balaclava, after the location of a Crimean War battle. (A charming ghost town in Renfrew County is also known as Balaklava.) Initially, the Irish settlers in Sheffield were proud to call their community Balaclava—it was a celebration of the exploits of their Irish brothers and sisters.

However, when the Crimean War was ancient history, the Irish grew tired of the long "foreign" name of Balaclava. And so, to shorten it, they simply called the community "Bala-heck," probably remembering the small Irish town Bally-hack (*Baile Shac* in Gaelic). While the change to Balaheck was accepted, the spelling of "Balaheck" was never established because the hamlet never had a post office. Depending on who you ask, Balaheck is spelled Balaheck, Balahac (like the Irish *Baile Shac*) or Baluhac. (The name is definitely not spelled "Bellheck," as was recorded by the Federal Geographic Names Secretariat.) Balaheck is pronounced BAL-uh-heck or BAL-uh-hack totally independently of how you spell it.

Confused? I am too!

BALENTRA. Balentra Station was a stop on the Nip & Tuck Railway about two kilometers south of Tamworth. (This same spot may also have been known locally as Wilson's Crossing.) Although the spelling has been altered, the name "Balentra" probably comes from the Scottish port town of Ballantrae, now part of Scotland's Strathclyde Region. In Scottish Gaelic, Ballantrae is, appropriately, "the village on the shore," though our Balentra Station wasn't on a body of water. The name is spelled Balentra and Balantra, the pronunciation changing appropriately ("bal-EHN-truh" and "bal-AHN-truh.") A development near Tamworth is now known as the Balantra subdivision.

CAWDOR. See Kaladar.

CLOYNE. An important village in northern Lennox & Addington, Cloyne is actually split between L & A's Anglesea Township and Frontenac's Barrie Township. Highway 41, Cloyne's main street, is the county line. The community has been called Cloyne (pronounced like "coin" with an added 'l') since 1859, when a post office was granted to the village. The name is another contribution from Ireland's County Cork, where the original Cloyne is known as the seat of an ancient Irish bishopric. In Gaelic, the town's name is *Cluain Uamha*, the "meadow of the caves."

COMER'S MILLS / VIOLET. Violet hamlet is in the northwestern part of Ernestown Township, just south of the 401. The community was first settled by United Empire Loyalists, including the Comer family, who owned a mill on Wilton (or Big) Creek. By 1853 the village had grown sufficiently for a post office, and in honour of the Comer family, the office was named Comer's Mills. In 1860, the community decided to rename the office in honor Mrs. Violet Comer, who had taken over her family's mill in spite of the overwhelming obstacles facing female entrepreneurs. Violet is one of the very few places in Eastern Ontario whose name specifically identifies a female pioneer—for other examples, see Cashion's Glen under Glengarry County and Aunt Sarah's Lookout under Haliburton County.

DENBIGH. The main service village for the northernmost part of Lennox & Addington County is Denbigh, now at the intersection of Highways 28 and 41. In spite of the community's large German population, the province picked a Welsh name for the town and surrounding township. Denbighshire was once a Welsh county, and there is still a town called Denbigh in the modern County Clwyd. The town's name means "the little fort" in Welsh, reflecting the presence of a nearby walled fort. The spelling of the name seems to throw people off the correct pronunciation, "DEHN-bee."

ENTERPRISE. Enterprise, in northern Camden East Township, started life as the cheekily named Shirt-Tail Corners (the reason for this name seems to be lost). Later, Shirt-Tail Corners became Thompson's Corners, for general store owner Robert Thompson. In 1854, the government refused to accept Thompson's Corners for use on the post office, insisting on something "more dignified." At a public meeting to discuss the question, the local schoolteacher, Mrs. Cox, is credited with having remarked how "enterprising" the residents were. Thompson (clearly something of a ham) then leapt dramatically onto a table to declare, "All other names we now despise, in support of Enterprise!" Enterprise stuck, and is still in use today.

FESTUBERT. Festubert P.O. is virtually forgotten today, now just a quiet cottage community in Anglesea Township. As historian Ross Oborne has written, local resident Mike Schwager applied for and received a post office there in 1927. He decided to name it "Festubert," after a French town where a battle was fought in the First World War. However, Schwager's fiancee refused to live in Schwager's island cottage-cum-post office, and so he had to give up the postmaster's job. It then fell to Mrs. Beatrice Yanch, who distributed the mail from her general store (called Royal Oak Cottage). After a family tragedy, Mrs. Yanch also retired, and so Festubert disappeared off the map.

GRETNA. The hamlet of Gretna has left behind a strange tale about its name. In 1863, local resident W. J. Mellow applied for a new post office. When his request was approved, he received a set of postal hammers intended for another post office. For some reason, that other office had never opened, and so (not wanting to be wasteful) the hammers were "recycled." Mellow was quoted as simply saying, "The stamps were sent here and I have used them ever since." Gretna, which is on the Napanee River in North Fredericksburgh Township, probably takes its name from a town in Dumfries & Galloway, Scotland. In Old English, a "gretna" is "a gravely hill."

KALADAR / CAWDOR. The origin of the name "Kaladar" has confounded historians and local residents for a century and a half. The name has appeared here since the township was surveyed in the 1820s, though no explanation of the origin has survived. Several theories have grown up since then: a popular (though not very plausible) story says the word is a corruption of "Kill a deer," which came about because deer were so plentiful in the area; historian Herbert Gardiner, in 1899, proposed it might come from the Spanish word for "heat" (suggested because one Upper Canadian governor had given Spanish names to Ontario townships); some believed "Kaladar" was an Irish village or estate. However, none of these stories could be substantiated.

The real origin of Kaladar was found in 1944, by a Gaelic linguist named Francis Diack. Diack spent years traveling through northeastern Scotland, collecting the Gaelic place-names of that region. These names were in popular use, but weren't official—they didn't appear on the maps. Among his discoveries, Diack identified the Gaelic name of Cawdor, a Scottish village and parish, as Caladir. Coincidentally, an early post office in Kaladar Township was named Cawdor, clinching the link between the two communities. It's possible a township resident or someone in the government recognized the Kaladar-Cawdor connection and named the post office Cawdor in 1865. If Diack hadn't recorded Caladir back in 1944, it likely would have been lost forever—the number of Gaelic speakers in Scotland has shrunk dramatically, and the old place-names are falling out of use.

LENS STATION. The peculiar name of this railway station in Camden East conjures up the image of an itinerant optometrist, but the name originally came from France. Lens is a small town near Calais, and saw heavy fighting during the First World War. The name might have ended up on this station because of Lens' connection with the railways—the French town contained a strategic railway connection, which the Germans had captured and used to supply their army with locally mined coal. After repeated attacks, the British captured Lens in 1918, which was around the time Lens Station was added to the Nip & Tuck line.

MASSANOGA / MAZINAW LAKE. These two places—the former a logging town in Effingham Township, the other a large lake on the Lennox & Addington/Frontenac border—both take their names from an aboriginal expression. The word *Muzinuhigun* means "picture" or "writing," a reference to the now-deteriorating aboriginal pictograms painted on Bon Echo rock. It's not certain which language *Muzinuhigun* comes from. The native Algonquin people of this area have indicated *Muzinuhigun* is not an Algonquin word. Wherever the name came from, it's been in use for more than a century. Early maps show Mazinaw Lake as "Massanoga Lake" or "Mishinog Lake," and the post office at the Bon Echo Hotel was dubbed Massanoga in 1902.

MILLHAVEN. Millhaven hamlet was a busy centre as early as 1795, when thirsty travelers stopped at Mrs. Losie's Tap Room for a pint. There are several explanations for the "Millhaven" name, which has become known across the country (perhaps unfairly) as the home of a maximum-security prison. Some people suggest it came about because the hamlet was literally a "haven for mills." Several businesses located here to take advantage of Millhaven Creek, and for years afterwards Millhaven was known as an industrial village. It's also possible the "haven" in mind is the hamlet's little harbor, which is one of the most sheltered spots along Ernestown's south shore. In either case, the name has been in continuous use for almost two hundred years.

POSTHAVEN. The area just north of the Skootamatta Lake side-road on Highway 41 is apparently known as "Posthaven." The only possible explanation I can think of is that this was once quite close to the old Festubert Post Office (see above) . . . therefore, a literal "post-haven." The name is extremely obscure and not mentioned in any printed source I could find.

ROB ROY. This curious post office name may have been used at one time in Lennox & Addington. Floreen Carter's *Ghost and Post Offices of Ontario* says the name appears in the records, but that it may have been a clerical error. There was another Rob Roy in Southwestern Ontario, so someone at the post office department may have put the name under the wrong county. The origin of the name is no mystery—*Rob Roy* is a novel by Sir Walter Scott, recording the exploits of a Scottish "Robin Hood"-like character. In the 1710s, a powerful duke seized Rob Roy's grazing lands seized to cover a minor debt. He raised an army to fight this persecution, and fought the propertied interests for more than twenty years.

ROGUES' HOLLOW. Early in its history, the village with the fairly sedate name of Newburgh had the delightful title "Rogues' Hollow." The name was descriptive in two ways: not only was Rogues' Hollow in the Napanee River valley, the community was renowned as a hotbed of sin. The village had several taverns—a serious matter in a strongly dry area—and, worse still, was home to several millers! (Truly hucksters of the first order.) Rogues' Hollow was "the heathen name," wrote one temperance crusader, "the Christian name is Newburgh." Newburgh was suggested by the local newspaper editor after he had visited Newburgh, N.Y. He thought the New York village a prosperous and progressive town, so when the post office opened in 1846, he proposed "Newburgh" as a dignified alternative to Rogues' Hollow. It's kind of a shame the people took up his suggestion, really. Wouldn't you detour off the 401 to see a town called Rogues' Hollow?!

THE ROUGH CAST SCHOOL. This bizarre name was given to a small school section in Ernestown Township, along the south shore of Parrotts Bay. The inspiration for the name wasn't a bratty pack of students, but probably the metal school bell, which had been imperfectly cast. Rough Cast, S.S. #3 of Ernestown, was later absorbed into the Millhaven school section.

SKOOTAMATTA RIVER. "The Skoot," as it's usually referred to, runs from Skootamatta Lake in Anglesea Township down to Stoco Lake at Tweed. The Skoot was regularly used for log drives in the 19th century, and logging continues on a small scale in the Skootamatta watershed. The word Skootamatta (pronounced "skoot-uh-MAT-uh") comes from the Huron language, and is said to mean "shooting star." Until quite recently, Skootamatta Lake was called simply "Loon Lake"—the aboriginal name was used to differentiate this lake from the many other Loon Lakes in Ontario.

STELLA. This is the main village on Amherst Island, encompassing the general store, the post office, and the bank. The village has been known as Stella since 1860, though the source of the name has never been discovered. (The same applies for the island's other village, Emerald, also named in 1860.) Local historian Tom Sylvester hypothesized that "Stella" might have been a female relative of a one-time owner of Amherst Island. It's also possible Stella—a heavily Irish community at one time—took its name from Ireland's most famous Stella. Esther "Stella" Johnston was the lover of Dean Swift, one of Ireland's most noted poets. Could a fan of Swift's have suggested "Stella" for the new post office in 1860?

VENNACHAR. Vennachar, a small community in Abinger Township, is remembered as the site of the devastating 1903 Vennachar Fire. The blaze, accidentally touched off by two farmers burning some brush, not only destroyed Vennachar but singed villages up to fifty kilometers away. The hamlet never recovered from the fire, but its story has given the village a prominent place in county history. While most of Vennachar's early settlers were German, the name "Vennachar" is Scottish—Loch Vennachar (pronounced, in Scotland and in Canada, "venn-ACK-ur") is a small lake in Scotland. The word is Gaelic in origin, and Loch Vennachar means "the lake of the mountain hills."

VIOLET. See Comer's Mills.

WESLEMKOON. Weslemkoon Lake is one of the largest lakes in this part of Ontario, and remains a beautiful cottage retreat. The name (pronounced "WEZ-lee-em-koon" or "wes-lem-uh-KOON") is an aboriginal word, which translates as the bizarre "running bank beaver." The image of a pudgy beaver travelling at high speed is pretty difficult to conjure up! Weslemkoon hamlet, at the lake's southern tip, can claim what may be the shortest-serving post office in Eastern Ontario history. The office opened at the home of Walter Kidd on 01 August 1928, and was axed by the government thirty days later. There's also a unique expression to describe a visit here—when residents in nearby Gunter and Gilmour talk about visiting Weslemkoon, the expression is "going up the 'Koon."

WESTPLAIN. The inspiration for the name of Westplain, in the northwestern corner of Richmond Township, is obvious to anyone who's been there: the hamlet sits on a perfectly-flat stretch of limestone and fields. Many people have mistaken the name as having to be two words (i.e., "West Plain") but local preference is just one word, "Westplain." Residents often referred to the hamlet as the "City on the Rocks" from its barren location.

WOODMUCKET. The tiny hamlet of Woodmucket is billed, jokingly, as a suburb of Yarker (also detailed in this chapter). The community takes in a few houses just south of Yarker, as well as a string of farms along the Napanee River. The origin of this delightful name—which doesn't appear on any map, and was never used on a post office—is a mystery, but there are several possibilities. One of the early settlers may have been thinking of the marshy Napanee River, "Woodmucket" having a decided marshy-sounding ring to it. It's also possible someone had heard of Woonsocket, Rhode Is., and got the name kind of garbled. Whatever the origin may be, Woodmucket is one of the most curious names in Eastern Ontario.

YARKER. Yarker hamlet, on the Napanee River in Camden East Township, has dined out for years on the story of its name. Back in the 1850s, the residents of what was then Simcoe Falls were asked to come up with a new name for their post office. (The land on which the village stands was once owned by Governor John Graves Simcoe, giving rise to the Simcoe Falls name.) At a public meeting, eight suggestions were drawn up, including "Peking," as in the capital of China, "Rockburg" and, at the bottom, "Yarker." The Yarkers were a German family of millwrights who didn't even live in town—they were from nearby Harrowsmith. For reasons known only to the postal bureaucrats, Yarker got the nod. In thanks, the flattered Yarkers donated a bell to the Yarker school.

YARKER
ON
KOK 3N0

13. Prince Edward County

Prince Edward is one of the least-populous counties in Eastern Ontario, with around 22 000 permanent residents. "The County" (as it is almost universally referred to along the Lake Ontario shore) is virtually a sandy island, bounded by Lake Ontario on the south and the Bay of Quinte on the north. Only a narrow isthmus at Carrying Place connects Prince Edward to the mainland, and even that link is divided by the Murray Canal. The obvious result of the geography is that Prince Edward has always relied on water transportation—more than any other Eastern Ontario County, Prince Edward has a maritime tradition which has shaped its lake shore place-names. Most of the inland villages are named for early Loyalist settlers, but a few communities are outside that traditional mold.

••❖••

BALD HEAD. Bald Head is a thin sandy spit that separates Wellers Bay from Lake Ontario. The name is a very old one with an obvious origin—the spit is almost devoid of vegetation, i.e., it's "bald." Names containing "Bald" can sometimes be traced back to a French description "pélée," meaning "bald" and usually referring to a treeless stretch of land. The famous Point Pelee in Southwestern Ontario is the most obvious example of this kind of name.

CAPE VESEY & POINT TRAVERSE. One of the many capes along South Marysburg's scalloped shoreline, Cape Vesey was originally known as Point Traverse. From 1865 until 1918, a South Marysburgh post office was also known as Point Traverse from this cape. However, the word "traverse" was eroded through use to just "vesey," and today the point is locally referred to as Cape Vesey. Some maps show Cape Vesey as just "The Rock."

CARRYING PLACE. This is one of the County's most distinctive names, designating a village right on the Prince Edward-Northumberland line. Like Twelve O'Clock Point (see Northumberland County) and Quinte (see below), Carrying Place is a name with roots back to New France. Before the Murray Canal linked the Bay of Quinte and Lake Ontario, people travelling by water had to portage across the isthmus between modern Prince Edward and Northumberland. As canoes were carried over the portage, the site became known as "the carrying place," and the local community simply adopted this name when it was settled by the Loyalists. (The local post office was known as Murray, after surrounding Murray Township, until "Carrying Place" was readopted in 1913.) The Carrying Place portage was used by the First Nations People for centuries, and became a strategic point during French rule—a military strong-hold, Fort Kenté, was constructed to defend the portage.

CONSECON. Consecon is located at the junction between Consecon Lake and Wellers Bay in Hillier Township. The village is one of the larger communities in the County, and was large enough to warrant its own post office by 1836. The word "consecon" is definitely aboriginal, though the meaning has not been precisely determined. Consecon may come from the Mississauga word for "pickerel," or from a longer phrase which means "an opening." Both meanings are suitable for Consecon—the village is right at the outlet of Consecon Lake, which is known as a good pickerel-fishing area. The name Consecon is pronounced with the emphasis on the first syllable ("CAWN-su-cawn").

CRESSY. The name Cressy had been used at several locations in North Marysburgh Township. The original Cressy P.O. opened near the eastern tip of the County in 1857, and moved to several different homes before being renamed Cressy East in 1913. At the same time, the post office at Bongard's Corners was inexplicably renamed Cressy for about three months in 1914. The confusion abruptly ended when every post office in North Marysburgh (with the exception of Waupoos) was closed in 1914. The name originally came from a North Marysburgh homestead called Cressy Farm. The Creasy family, owners of the farm, gave rise to the "Cressy" name.

DEMORESTVILLE. The name of this Sophiasburgh Township village causes some confusion for folks from away, as local pronunciation places the emphasis on the third syllable, i.e., dem-oar-EST-ville. This local usage is a hold-over from the name's French origin—Guillaume De Morest was the first settler in this district, and one of the first European settlers to reach the County. In French, there is a slight accent on the "-rest" portion of De Morest's name, which has been maintained. However, in English, the name "De Morest" often comes out sounding like "forest," and Demorestville is frequently mispronounced "de-MOR-est-ville" as a result. The name first appeared on a local post office in 1829.

FALSE DUCKS ISLAND. Tiny False Ducks Island, just off Long Point in South Marysburgh, owes its name to early navigators on Lake Ontario. Much further out in Lake Ontario, about midway between the County and Upper New York State, are a pair of islands known as the Ducks. One of the pair has a lighthouse to guide lake traffic through the tricky waters around the County. This lighthouse still had a resident lighthouse keeper well into the 1960s. However, in the days before modern instrumentation and mapping, the two little islands off Long Point could be (and sometimes were) mistaken for the "real" Ducks Islands out in the lake. Well over a hundred ships have foundered or sunk near the County because of navigational errors like that one. The potential confusion between the two groups of islands inspired the name "False Ducks" for one of the two islands just off Long Point. In counterpoint, the lighthouse-equipped island became known as "Main Duck."

GLENORA. Glenora is often the first name people see when they come to the County. The hamlet is the terminus for the Adolphus Reach ferries, which connect the two halves of Highway 33 in Lennox & Addington and Prince Edward Counties. (One of the current ferries is also called the *Glenora*.) The name has a Scottish ring to it, but cannot be traced directly to Scotland. There is a Scottish valley called Glen Orrin and a Scottish community called Glenlora, but no Glenora. To find Glenora, we have to go back to the family of one of the area's first settlers, Loyalist Peter Vanalstine. Vanalstine built a milling operation here around 1800, and as a result the site of present-day Glenora was first known as Stone Mills. Years later, one of Vanalstine's relatives took over the operation—this relative had married one of Vanalstine's daughters, whose name was Glenora. When the community received a post office in 1893, her name was given to the office, and has remained in use ever since.

HUYCK'S POINT. This popular beach is down the dead-end County Road 20 in Hillier Township. The name, which is pronounced "HIKES," comes from a local Dutch settler, Andrew C. Huyck. Many of the Loyalists who fled from New York State were of Dutch descent, and these Loyalists account for some of the more unusual names around Eastern Ontario. Huyck's Point is bordered by Huyck's Bay to the north—another Huyck, Huyck's Road, can be found in South Fredericksburgh Township, Lennox & Addington County.

MUSCOTE BAY. This shallow bay runs south from the Bay of Quinte into Sophiasburgh Township, separating Big Island from the Prince Edward mainland. The well-known aboriginal name of Muscote Bay is said "mus-COAT-ee," another tricky County pronunciation. Muscote can probably be traced back to an aboriginal expression recorded by linguist Percy Robinson—apparently, the Mississauga people referred to this location as *maskoodaang*, meaning "at the meadows." The Mississaugas had picked up and translated an older name used by the Iroquois people (see Quinte, below). Over time, "maskoodaang" corrupted into "Muscote."

POINT PETRE. Point Petre, the southernmost point of the county, is another Prince Edward place name with a quirky pronunciation. The spelling of the name points the pronunciation "PEE-tree," and official marine weather reports refer to this Athol Township location as PEE-tree. However, some local residents call the cape Point "PEE-ter," which refers back to the original name of neighboring Soup Harbor, St. Peter's Bay. This name was one of the first given to Prince Edward's many bays, and remained in use until a memorable incident gave rise to Soup Harbor (see below). It's not known how "Peter" became "Petre," although it's not unusual for words with an "-re" ending (like metre, etc.) to be pronounced like the name "Peter." The change in spelling is also a mystery.

POINT TRAVERSE. See Cape Vesey.

QUINTE. "Quinte" is one of Eastern Ontario's oldest place-names, having been handed down through nearly four hundred years of recorded history. When the Iroquois saw the marshy and low-lying shoreline of the Bay of Quinte—separating Hastings from Prince Edward Counties—they called it *kenta* or *kahenta*, "a meadow." (The Iroquois word also travelled to the American South, where it gave rise to the name of Kentucky State.) When the traders of New France reached the bay area, they heard the name and transcribed it as Kenté. Later, the French built a stronghold to control the Carrying Place portage (see above) and called it Fort Kenté after the bay. This name was inscribed on the maps of New France, and subsequently passed on to the Loyalist settlers in the 18th century. Since then, "Kenté" has corrupted into "Quinte," which you'll often hear without a "t," i.e., "QUIN-ee," in local conversation. Prince Edward County is often referred to as "Quinte's Isle" from its location on the bay.

ROSSMORE. The village of Rossmore used to be a small fishing village in Ameliasburgh Township. Now that Rossmore is connected to Belleville by the Bay Bridge, suburban development is beginning to surround the original village. The name "Rossmore" is from a place near Poole, Dorsetshire, England—in Old English, a "rossmore" is a "marshy headland." The name may have been given to our Rossmore in 1876 because of its similarity to the English Rossmore. The Dorsetshire coast is low-lying and swampy, as is the south shore of the Bay of Quinte. Originally, our Rossmore was spelled as two words ("Ross More").

SCOHARIE ROAD. Prince Edward Road 1, which runs from Consecon right across the county to Picton, is called "the Scoharie Road." There's little doubt the name was brought by the Loyalists from New York State—a county in the Mohawk Valley of Upper New York is called Scoharie. The county (established in 1795) takes its name from a Mohawk word meaning "driftwood." Scoharie is said "scoh-HAIR-ee."

SCOTCH BONNET. Scotch Bonnet is a tiny rocky islet off the southwest coast of Hillier Township. The island was so bleak that when a lighthouse was built here in the early 1800s, the first lighthouse keeper refused to live there—the conditions were impossible to take, he said. The name "Scotch Bonnet" has no obvious inspiration, although the rocky island does resemble the most barren parts of the Scottish Highlands.

SHEBA'S ISLAND. This little island in West Lake is now a popular resort area. The name seems to have a Biblical connection (as in the Queen of Sheba), but is really about 2 000 years more recent than that. The island subdivision was started by Toronto developer Michael Sheba, and his name was later used in place of the then-current usage, "Wynne's Island." Earlier still, Sheba's had been called Tubbs' Island.

SOUP HARBOR. This wide bay separates Point Petre from Wicked Point (see below) in Athol Township. The bay was originally called St. Peter's Bay (see Point Petre, above), but a notable shipwreck inspired a name change. Sometime in the 1800s, a ship carrying a load of barley upset and sank in the bay, spilling the cargo into the lake. With bushels of barley in the water, some wit coined the name "Soup Harbor," which has been in use ever since.

WAUPOOS. There are several places in the County bearing this name, including Waupoos proper, Waupoos East, and Waupoos Island, which once had its own ferry service. The name dates back to at least 1871, when Waupoos village was granted a post office. The word "waupoos" is aboriginal in origin, and is said to mean "rabbit" in the Mississauga language. There's no explanation given as to why Waupoos was applied to this place. It's possible the name is from the same era as Carrying Place (see above), when First Nations People still moved freely throughout the County.

WICKED POINT. Better known as Salmon Point, Wicked Point is a wide cape at the southwestern tip of Athol Township. Anyone who's sailed the waters off Prince Edward will tell you the reason for the name—this stretch of the lake is notorious for hidden shoals and hard navigating. Many ships have gone to the bottom trying to get out of Athol Bay and around Wicked Point to Soup Harbor.

WOODROUS. Woodrous is shown at the intersection of County Roads 10 and 11 in Athol Township. However, the name ought not to be there, because it's a mistake. When a post office first opened in the hamlet in 1879, it was called Woodrow's, after the first postmaster, John Woodrow. However, a bureaucrat in the post office department misread this name as Woodrous, and the official postmark was subsequently made up as Woodrous. This is only one example of how bad penmanship has influenced the place-names of Eastern Ontario. (See Ossa under Frontenac County for more fun and games.)

YEREXVILLE. The eye-catching name of Yerexville hamlet stands at a Y-junction of roads just northwest of Picton. There was never a post office at that location, the name evolving through local usage in Hallowell Township. The source of the name is not in doubt, as several families named Yerex settled in the county and in neighboring Hastings. But if you ask directions to "YARE-uks-ville," as the name is written, you'll probably get a blank look— Yerexville is properly pronounced "YURKS-ville."

14. Hastings County

Hastings is a large, rectangular county, encompassing fully twenty-four townships from the Bay of Quinte to the Upper Madawaska Valley. About half the population lives in two lakeshore cities, Belleville and Trenton, with vast stretches of uninhabited territory north of Highway 7. The Tyendinaga First Nation (known as Kahnien:ke to the Mohawk people) is at the county's southeastern corner, and was one of the first Loyalist settlements in Eastern Ontario. (The Mohawks were staunch allies of the British during the American Revolution.) The townships near the Bay of Quinte have a definite Loyalist/Anglo bent to their names, but the mix is more varied the further north you go. The county's name remembers one of the most famous battles in English history—in a.d. 1066, William of Normandy defeated the Saxon King, Harold Godwinson, and conquered the island of Britain. William became King William I and founded the royal family we still have with us today. Hastings later became the surname of a wealthy English family, and one Francis Rawdon Hastings, Marquis of Hastings and Earl of Moira (1754-1826) is credited as the official inspiration for "Hastings County."

ACTINOLITE. The hamlet of Actinolite is near the intersection of Highways 37 and 7 in Elzevir Township. This community owes its existence to Senator Billa Flint, a wealthy and powerful lumber baron who controlled huge stretches of Eastern Ontario in the mid-19th century. He established a milling operation here under the name Troy, but the rapidly growing settlement became known as Bridgewater P.O. in 1858. (The name was given because of a bridge over the Skootamatta River near town.) Lumbering remained the chief industry until the discovery of local deposits of actinolite—a green, jade like mineral which is officially known as calcium iron hydrous silicate. Mining quickly took off, and by 1895 the town had been renamed "Actinolite" in honor of the discovery.

ASTRA. Astra Post Office is the mailing address for the troops stationed at CFB Trenton. The office was originally called just "RCAF Station Trenton," but in October, 1966, the name was changed to Astra. The word means "stars" in Latin, and might have come from the air force's motto: Per Ardua ad Astra, "through adversity to the stars." Astra P.O. is located in Sidney Township.

BATAWA. This curious name appears on a village between Trenton and Frankford. Pronounced "BAT-uh-wuh," the community is a subdivision created in the 1940s by the Bata Shoe Company. Thomas Bata, a Hungarian businessman who fled the Nazi invasion of his country, relocated his shoe empire to North America around that time. Bata decided to build a plant in Sidney Township, and invented the name "Batawa" for the subdivision where his employees would live. Batawa P.O. opened in 1943 and survived until the most recent round of office closures. Even though the Batawa name is a recent addition to the landscape, local residents fought Canada Post to the wall to retain their postal address as "Batawa." They won, and the community intends to keep the Batawa name on the map.

BIRD'S CREEK. This hamlet is located just north of Bancroft in Herschel Township. Alan Rayburn reports the community was named in the 1800s for one of the men overseeing construction of the Hastings Road. As he was crossing the creek during construction, he slipped and fell in. Once safely back on shore, he decided to christen the creek "Bird's Creek" for himself. This name was later picked up by a local post office in 1885.

BONARLAW. "Bonarlaw" was the third name applied to a small rural post office in Rawdon Township. The office had first opened as Big Springs in 1884, changing to the uninspired "Bellview" in 1910. In 1920, the community underwent another name change to Bonarlaw, in honor of an English prime minister. (One story says the local railway company lobbied to have Bellview changed to Bonarlaw.) Andrew Bonar Law was a Conservative prime minister of the U.K. from 1922 until 1923, and a minister in several other cabinets. His career was watched closely in Canada because Bonar Law was an expatriate Canadian—he was born in Kingston, New Brunswick, and lived in Canada until age twelve. The name is pronounced with the emphasis on the first syllable, i.e., "BON-ur-law."

CORBYVILLE. The looming, red-brick buildings of Corby's Distillery can still be seen at Corbyville, even though—sadly—Corby's is now history. The Corby family grew wealthy on their successful distilling business, located here to use water from the Moira River. The old railway line, on which thousands of gallons of booze were shipped out, still bisects the village. When the post office opened in 1882, it was only natural for local residents to choose "Corbyville" for the name. Corbyville is now a prosperous-looking suburb of the city.

DELORO. See Eldorado.

ELDORADO & DELORO. Eldorado is a sleepy village on Highway 62 today, but a century ago it was briefly the centre of a frenzied gold rush in central Hastings County. Thousands of prospectors streamed into Madoc Township in the mid-1800s, looking to get rich quick. To serve this sudden throng, the government opened a post office in this instant mining town in 1867. Appropriate to the gold rush, the office was named Eldorado, after the mythical land of gold the Spanish believed they would find in South America.

Similarly, the Marmora Township community of Deloro appeared overnight during the rush. The name Deloro, meaning "valley of gold" in Spanish, was chosen for the community's post office in 1881. Although the mines (and Deloro Post Office) are long gone, the names Eldorado and Deloro remain here to remind people of the Hastings Gold Rush. Deloro is now one of the smallest incorporated villages in Ontario, with a population of about two hundred people.

ELZEVIR. The Township of Elzevir is in central Hastings, right along the Highway 7 corridor. In the mid-19th century, the township was the personal fiefdom of Senator Billa Flint (see Actinolite) who created the villages of Flinton and Bancroft. The township was named back in 1820, long before Flint arrived there. Curiously, "Elzevir" honors a family of Dutch printers—for almost two hundred years, the Elzevirs were famous throughout Europe for their extremely accurate work. The family included about a dozen different printers and publishers, including probably the world's first female publisher, Eva Elzevir. She was also the first woman to become an official university publisher when she was named printer to Leiden University, Holland, in 1661. The emphasis falls on the first syllable of the name ("EL-zuh-veer.") From 1908 to 1938, there was also a rural post office called simply Elzevir P.O. in the township.

FORT STEWART. This village is in the southern concessions of Carlow Township, near the Carlow-Mayo line. Traditionally, the hamlet's name has been credited to an early tavern-keeper in Carlow, John Stewart. However, given that Carlow is an Irish name, it's possible Fort Stewart P.O. was named for the town of Fort Stewart in Ireland. This explanation lacks some logic, as Fort Stewart is in County Donegal, not County Carlow—perhaps our Fort Stewart was named in echo of the Irish community and to honor John Stewart. The name was coined in February 1891.

FOXBORO. One of the largest rural villages in Hastings, Foxboro has become home for many commuters working in the city of Belleville. The town was originally known as Smithville, though another Smithville in Southwestern Ontario forced a change of name in 1861. The inspiration for "Foxboro" has been something of a mystery—the reasons for the choice seem to have been lost since 1861. In the 1851 Census of Thurlow Township, a Mrs. Mary Fox, widow, is reported living in Smithville with her children Patrick, Bridget, James, Margaret, Mary, Thomas, Michael, Sarah, Catherine, Henrietta, and John (eleven in all). It's possible the post office was named Foxboro for this family, through there's no obvious reason for the choice. There is another Foxboro, in the northwestern corner of the State of Wisconsin. However, it's unlikely that area had even been settled when our Foxboro was named. Three generations of the Fox family in England were leading politicians in the 18th and 19th centuries. Two of the Foxes were contemporaries of Francis Rawdon Hastings, for whom Hastings County is named (see the introduction to this chapter). The name "Fox" may have become known in Smithville through some connection between the Hastings and Fox families.

HARTSMERE. This lonely hamlet is several kilometres south of Highway 28 in Mayo Township. Until the Snow Road was constructed through the township around the mid-19th century, settlement was virtually impossible in this rugged, inaccessible area. After the Snow Road was complete, a hamlet sprang up at the intersection where Hartsmere now stands. The community was first given the descriptive name "Deer Meadow," and then renamed "Hartsmere P.O." in 1881. It's possible Hartsmere was invented from the original name Deer Meadow—a male deer is a "hart," and the word "mere" is sometimes applied to meadows or open areas in England. There is also a place in central England called Hertsmere which is pronounced just like Hartsmere. "Hertsmere" means "the boundary land of Hertfordshire" in Old English, the village lying right on the boundary between Hertfordshire and Berkshire. The Snow Road has largely disintegrated, but Hartsmere lives on as the township seat of Mayo.

HAVERGAL. The Carlow Township hamlet of Havergal is almost a ghost town today. The name was chosen by the local postmaster, John Campbell, who was an avid reader of American poet Frances Ridley Havergal. Campbell and his successors operated Havergal P.O. from 1886 until 1929. Previously, the office had been known as Conroy's Farm (1879-1886) for the then-postmaster.

HERMON & UPPER HERMON. Two communities in Mayo Township—Hermon and Upper Hermon—took the name of the Biblical Mount Hermon. The mountain is now part of Lebanon, still under its original name. The Canadian Hermon sprang up where the old Snow Road crossed a short, connecting route to the Peterson Colonization Road. The post office was established in 1878 just north of this crossing, and slowly Hermon proper moved to this new site. The old hamlet, which has now totally disappeared, became known as "Upper Hermon." Both communities are often shown as "Herm_a_n," as in the male Christian name—however, no notable Herman seems to have any connection to this area.

HYBLA. This hamlet in Monteagle Township is one of the few in Eastern Ontario that can trace its name to Italy. (See also Lodi under Stormont County and Buzztown under Frontenac.) The original Italian town of Hybla is noted for its bee-keepers and good quality honey. Our Hybla was a mining town on the old Central Ontario Railway—a feldspar mine here provided steady work during the inter-war years. Hybla P.O. opened in 1879, and survived until 1955, when Hybla's population had dwindled to a few families. The Central Ontario has been replaced by a hiking trail between Hybla and Graphite, to the north.

IVANHOE. Ivanhoe on Highway 62 is home to one of Hastings' last surviving cheese factories, and is the municipal seat for Huntingdon Township. Students of English literature will recognize the name immediately—one of the novels of Sir Walter Scott was called *Ivanhoe*. The title character of the book, published in 1819, is an English knight in the Middle Ages. Ivanhoe is one of several villages in Eastern Ontario named for the works of Scott (see also Lammermoor under Lanark County). The community was originally known as St. George-Hastings, the "Hastings" added to differentiate the village from St. George-Brant in Southwestern Ontario.

KAMANISKEG LAKE. Convoluted Kamaniskeg Lake twists across both Bangor Township in Hastings and Renfrew's Sherwood Township. Surveyor David Thompson, the first European to see the lake, identified it on his 1837 map as "We-Mine-Tik-Oos"—this is said to be an aboriginal phrase meaning "the lake of many islands." Later surveyors named the lake "Kamaniskeg," also an aboriginal word, meaning "wild goose." Alan Rayburn reports "Kamaniskeg Lake" can be found on maps as far back as 1847. In the mid-19th century, Canada geese were thick in the air in Eastern Ontario, and the name Kamaniskeg was probably a reflection of this fact. Kamaniskeg is usually said "kam-un-IS-keg."

L'AMABLE. This name is applied to a village and a small lake just south of Bancroft. Like nearby Paudash (see below), L'Amable takes its name from an aboriginal family who once lived and trapped in this area. While the surname is French (meaning "the amiable or likable one"), the French pronunciation has been simplified from "lam-AHB-luh" to "lam-AHB." L'Amable Post Office opened in Dungannon Township in 1869. The hamlet now called Detlor was also known as "L'Amable Station" from 1902 to 1904. L'Amable Lake, which forced the old Hastings Road to detour east from its planned route, is in Faraday Township.

LOST CHANNEL. The intriguing name of Lost Channel is found just south of Stoco Lake in Hungerford Township. The hamlet is in a tangle of streams which forms the upper part of the Moira River. An old story says that, when a log driver was guiding a raft of timber through here, he became confused because of the three different branches of the river. For that reason, he called the spot "Lost Channel." The name was later given to a post office on Hungerford's 6th Line in 1889. The office closed in 1899, but the location is still known as Lost Channel in the area.

MAYNOOTH, TARA & OXENDEN. "Ma-NOOTH," as it is usually said, is in Monteagle Township, a short distance north of Bancroft. The village fits in with the strongly Irish flavor of the place-names here—the original Maynooth, pronounced slightly differently from its Canadian cousin ("ma-NOOAT"), is a community in County Cork. The name means "Nuadha's Plain," honoring a ruler of the ancient Kingdom of Munster. Prior to being named Maynooth in 1863, the Monteagle village went by two other names. The first post office was granted as Tara in 1861, taking the name of a hill in County Meath. Tara (meaning "the hill homestead") was revered as a sacred place by the ancient Celts. For some reason, Tara P.O. then became Oxenden P.O. for exactly four months in early 1863. There are at least two places of this name in England (Great Oxendon in Northamptonshire, and Oxenton in Gloucestershire), both meaning "the hill where oxen are pastured." Oxenden was replaced by Maynooth on 01 April 1863, and Maynooth is the only name recognized there today.

MOIRA. One of Eastern Ontario's larger rivers is the Moira, which flows from Stoco Lake at Tweed south into Belleville. The river's name is often mispronounced by leaving out the "o"—Moira is properly said as "MWI-ruh," not "MI-ruh." Many of the major place-names in south Hastings, including Moira, can be traced to one-time British prime minister Francis Hastings. The townships of Rawdon, Huntingdon, and Hungerford all take their names from his family, and among his titles was the Earldom of Moira. Thurlow and Sidney, two other townships here, were named after cabinet colleagues of Hastings. Before European settlement, the Moira was known as the Sagonaska to the First Nations people. A Moira Post Office served residents in south Huntingdon Township from 1841 to 1968.

MUSCLOW. Musclow village is in the southern concessions of Monteagle Township, a few kilometres east of Bird's Creek. The Musclow family were early settlers in this area, and one E. Musclow was appointed the first postmaster of this village in 1910. The curious surname Musclow is pronounced with the emphasis on the first syllable, "MUS-clow."

OXENDEN. See Maynooth.

PAUDASH. The community of Paudash is on Highway 28, at the eastern tip of Lower Paudash Lake. There is also a larger Paudash Lake in neighboring Cardiff Township. All three are named for an aboriginal chief, Pahtosh (or Paudash), reputed to have lived in the Kawartha district before European settlement. The village had postal service until 1948, while a second "Paudash Lake P.O." existed for a few months in 1888.

ST. OLA. St. Ola (pronounced "OH-luh") is on the 2nd Line of Limerick, near the village of Gunter. Tradition says St. Ola took its name from a small Scottish church—local settler Peter Clark, a Scottish expatriate, made the choice in 1869 for the hamlet's new post office. The saint honored is Olaf, a Viking and the King of Norway until his death in a.d. 1030. There were hundreds of Viking settlements in eastern Scotland and England, and it's not unusual to find the names of Norwegian saints in that area. St. Ola P.O. closed in 1970, almost exactly one hundred years after it opened.

SHANNONVILLE. This village is surrounded by the Tyendinaga Reserve, about half-way between Napanee and Belleville. The land was leased from the Mohawks of Tyendinaga in 1819, through a long-simmering dispute over the ownership of the property has only recently been resolved. The land was on a good water-power site on the Salmon River, and as early as the 1820s Shannonville was a growing mill town. The community's name was given in 1833, when Shannonville received one of the first post offices in Hastings. (This office is still in operation more than 160 years later.) According to tradition, the name Shannonville was either chosen for or by the Port family, who had come from the valley of Ireland's great Shannon River.

SINE. Named for a local family of Dutch settlers, Sine is at the junction of Highway 14 and the 5th Line of Rawdon. Brothers Peter and William Sine took up a land grant here in the early 1800s, and a large group of family members followed them over from Holland. Their family name persisted here and was given to a post office in 1885.

STOCO. Stoco Lake is in the northwestern part of Hungerford—the town of Tweed is on the lake's western shore. A village and former railway station at the southern tip of the lake also took the name Stoco in the 19th century. According to tradition, "Stoco" is derived from Stougcong, the name of a powerful Mississauga chief. During the early days of European settlement, Stougcong led his people up the Moira (which they knew as the Sagonaska) to fish and trap. Stoco is pronounced with two long "o"s, i.e. "STOE-coe."

SULPHIDE. The largely deserted village of Sulphide got its name from the area's sulfuric acid industry. The village, in the northeastern part of Hungerford Township, was created during the Hastings Gold Rush (see Eldorado, above). Little gold was ever found here, but in 1905 an acid plant was built to exploit the local supply of sulfurous pyrites. The mine closed in 1964, and most of the residents moved away—the name of Sulphide still survives. The straggly remains of the Lakeshore Line railway running from Sulphide through to Kaladar (see Lennox & Addington County) are known as "the Sulphide Road."

TARA. See Maynooth.

THANET. Thanet was one of many failed farming hamlets along the central section of the Hastings Colonization Road. The village—of which only the cemetery remains—was between Murphys Corners and Ormsby, on the Wollaston-Limerick townline. The village's primary function was as a stopping place, where travellers could refresh themselves at three different hotels. When local farming failed, the village disappeared. The name "Thanet" is taken from the easternmost tip of England—during the Middle Ages, this sandy point was separated from the mainland by a narrow channel (since silted in). The English called the point the Isle of Thanet, taken from the Roman name Tanatus. Scholars believe Tanatus was based on a Celtic word for "bright," used here because the Romans had built their famous Pharos (lighthouse) of Dover on the island. Our Thanet was named in 1865, probably because the English Thanet is near the English Hastings.

TUFTSVILLE. This hamlet is right on the Sidney-Rawdon townline, a few kilometres east of Stirling village. The name "Tuftsville" was inspired by a local family, the Tufts, who settled the town line area in the early 19th century. From 1884 to 1913, the community had its own post office.

UMFRAVILLE. Like Thanet, Umfraville was a short-lived community on the Hastings Colonization Road. The hamlet was on the Dungannon Township section of the road, just south of L'Amable Lake. Umfraville—approved as the post office name in 1864—was the surname of a Scottish noble family, the Earls of Angus. These earls were actually Norman warriors, sent by the Norman kings of England to subdue the rebellious Scots. The Umfravilles (who hailed from a village of that name in France's La Manche region) did their duty and suppressed the Scots, until the Umfraville family eventually died out in 1436. The Scottish settlers on North Hastings may have been familiar with the old Earls of Angus, and given the name "Umfraville" from that connection.

UPPER HERMON. See Hermon.

15. Northumberland County

Northumberland is one of the largest counties in Eastern Ontario by population, taking in a stretch of the Lake Ontario shoreline between Trenton and Port Hope. Unlike its neighbors, Northumberland does not intrude onto the sparsely populated Canadian Shield, with its scattered logging towns and rugged landscape. Instead, the county is heavily agricultural, with many sizable towns located close to one another along the lake shore. The inspiration for the name "Northumberland" comes from the county's rolling hills, which contrast sharply with the mostly flat landscape of the rest of Eastern Ontario. In the 1790s, when Governor John Graves Simcoe was naming Eastern Ontario's counties, this area reminded him of the hilly terrain in Northumberland back in England. The town and village names of our Northumberland, however, are rarely English, being a curious grab-bag of names from all over the world. In this sense, too, Northumberland is distinct from most other counties in this book.

BALTIMORE. The name "Baltimore" is not particularly unusual, but its origin has long been debated in this Hamilton Township village. There's no argument the original Baltimore is Irish—in the 16th century, a minor British noble was given the title of Baron Baltimore and with it a large parcel of land in County Cork. The title was taken from the village *Baile na Tighe Mór*, whose name means the "homestead of the mansion" in Gaelic. (The community is still called Baltimore in English, but its Irish name has been changed to *Dún na Séad*, "the fort of the jewels.") The name travelled across the Atlantic to the U.S., where a large Maryland city is now called Baltimore. Similarly, a North American bird was named the Baltimore Oriole because the bird's plumage is the same colors as the Baltimore family crest (orange and black).

Our Canadian Baltimore may have taken its name directly from Ireland, as the village is near the hamlet of Skibbereen (see below), another likely Irish place name brought here by Irish settlers. While many of Northumberland's early inhabitants could trace their origins to the northeastern U.S., it seems no settlers from Maryland—who would have known the Baltimore name from their home state—made it to Hamilton Township. There's even an old tale the name was picked up after a drunk wandered into the village and thought it was Baltimore,

Maryland. (He must have been *very* drunk.) The "Irish settlers" version seems to be the most likely, given the presence of Skibbereen.

THE BREAKAWAY. This well-known landmark is just northwest of Hilton in Brighton Township. The name came about because of a memorable accident in 1862—there are several versions of the story, but the basic facts are pretty well established. In the 1860s, there were two competing mill-owners working in this part of the township. Eventually, one decided he would ruin the other by destroying the mill dam holding back Little (sometimes called Hilton or Cedar) Lake. At night, during a major downpour, the one mill-owner crept out to the other's mill-pond and poured in a large amount of quicksilver (mercury). Back then, it was believed quicksilver caused water to expand, and by adding the quicksilver the one mill-owner believed his competitor's pond would overflow its dam.

As a result of the quicksilver or the heavy downpour, the mill-pond did just that. However, the effect was far more devastating than planned: the dam holding back the lake burst, and a huge tidal wave ripped through the narrow valley of what is now Breakaway Creek. Two people were killed as the water destroyed a wide area below the dam, washing away tons of sand. This catastrophe became known as "The Breakaway of Hilton Creek," and its effects can still be seen in the valley carved by the floodwaters.

CAMBORNE. Camborne village is a few kilometres north of Cobourg in Hamilton Township. The name's origin seems to have eluded some researchers, but like Penryn (see below), Camborne can be traced back to central Cornwall. The original Camborne is located near Truro, barely a stone's throw from Penryn. In Cornish, *camborne* (a combination of *cam* and *bron*) means "the place by the curving slope," describing its location on the rugged Cornish peninsula. The name was brought here by the district's first settler—William Hore came from the Cornish Camborne to settle in Northumberland.

CANKERVILLE. Cankerville no longer appears on the official Ontario road map, but its name (popularized by poet Diane Dawber in her 1984 book *Cankerville*) is still well known in Brighton Township. The origin of this bizarre name goes back to the earliest days of settlement in Northumberland. Sometime in the 1790s, an official Land Agent—a government official charged with distributing free land to new settlers—arrived in Brighton Township to begin his work. However, when he arrived, he found a group of Irish squatters had already begun farming on some of the land he was to distribute. When asked, they refused to leave, claiming squatters' rights. Despite repeated efforts, the Land Agent could not persuade, force, or otherwise cajole these farmers into leaving. In frustration, he yelled that these farmers "were like a canker sore" because they simply would not go away. The farmers did not yield, and ever since the area has been known as Cankerville. The exact limits of the hamlet, which is just off Highway 30, were described in an old rhyme: "From Pat's Creek to Richmond's Mill/Is the extent of Cankerville." The mill is long since gone and the creek has been renamed, but the original rhyme is still known in the township.

CAT HOLLOW (LAKEPORT). You won't find Cat Hollow on the map, but for decades it was the local nickname of Lakeport hamlet in Cramahe Township. There has been some speculation about where the name might have come from, but so far there's no definitive answer. It's possible at some point there was an incident involving a bobcat or lynx in the village—in the early 19th century, these wild animals would undoubtedly have ranged further south more frequently than they do today. Lakeport has always been the official name, the local post office operating under that name until 1970.

CRAMAHE. This name of this township in eastern Northumberland stands out among the mostly English township names in this county. Cramahe, which is pronounced "CRAM-ee," was named to honor a Swiss-born Canadian politician, Hector Theophilus Cramahe. In 1770, Cramahe became the administrator (essentially the acting governor) of Québec when the Governor, Baron Dorchester, was out of the country. Dorchester remained overseas for four years, during which time Cramahe prepared the colony for the Québec Act (1774)—that law established the fundamental civil rights of Québec francophones to retain their identity. Despite his lengthy tenure, Cramahe's name does not appear on the official list of Canadian governors and governors-general. Cramahe Township was created and named in 1792, when most of the other lakeshore townships in Northumberland were laid out.

GANARASKA RIVER. The Ganaraska, which once had the dull name Smiths Creek, flows southwest from the Town of Newcastle, through Hope Township, and into Lake Ontario at Port Hope. The name was taken from a Mississauga community that stood at the river mouth when French fur traders first reached this area. According to linguist Percy Robinson, the name "Ganara-ske" means "where the fish spawn" in Mississauga, referring to the incredible salmon run that used to fill the Ganaraska. "As late as 1773," he writes, "the salmon came in from the sea in such numbers that the [fur] trader's dog could fish for himself." The distinctive Ganaraska name was temporarily displaced by Smiths Creek (for a local settler) in the 1820s, but Ganaraska has been in regular use since then. Local residents often refer to the river as "the Ganny."

GODOLPHIN. The hamlet of Godolphin is in a small valley in Percy Township, a few kilometres south of Hastings village. The name is Cornish, another of the unusually large number of Cornish place-names in Northumberland County. The Godolphins were an English noble family who owned a huge estate in Cornwall. One of the Godolphins was appointed governor of the Scilly Islands, a tiny, rocky archipelago off the southwestern tip of Cornwall. Another Godolphin was involved in the breeding of the Godolphin Arabian, a popular riding horse. Two villages in Cornwall—Godolphin Cross and Godolphin Hill—have taken the name of their former noble owners. When our Godolphin P.O. opened in 1886, the Godolphins were still prominent in English government and politics.

GOSPORT. The former fishing village of Gosport has now become a sizable suburb of nearby Brighton. Gosport still has a strong connection to the lake, as there is a marina located nearby. The hamlet was created by a government-sponsored subdivision plan in the 1880s, and it's possible the name "Gosport" is a contraction of "GOvernment-SPonsored pORT." There is also a town called Gosport in England's Hampshire—the community's name comes from Old English and means the "geese market," i.e., the market where geese are sold. The town is most famous as the launching point from which Canada's soldiers left for France on D-Day. The first "o" in Gosport is short ("GAWS-port").

HOARD'S STATION. This one-time railway hamlet still survives in southwestern Seymour Township, even though the railway disappeared years ago. The name Hoard's Station is still heard frequently throughout eastern Northumberland, as this is the site of the local livestock auction. The original station was built on land owned by the Hoard family, who farmed several lots in this area. The name is also shown without an apostrophe (i.e., Hoards Station) or simply Hoards, though this is not the most common local usage. From 1883 to 1946, Hoard's Station had its own post office.

LOUGHBREEZE. The strange name Loughbreeze appears on some detailed maps of Northumberland County, but the community isn't referred to in any of the older documentary sources. The name must have been coined very recently, even as late as the 1950s. The hamlet is on a small natural harbor, almost due south of Colborne on the lake shore. Possibly Loughbreeze was a seasonal fishing village at one time, as the harbor would have encouraged people to settle on this otherwise-isolated spot. The name Loughbreeze may have been chosen by an Irish settler, as in Irish, a lake is known as a *lough*. "Loughbreeze," therefore, means "lake breeze," an appropriate name for this lakeside community.

MENIE. Menie (pronounced "MIN-ee") is on the 5th Line of Seymour Township, just north of Hoard's Station (see above). A Scottish expatriate probably chose Menie for this post office in 1857—there is a mansion called Menie House and a village called Menie Links in the Grampian Region of Scotland. Despite the hamlet's small size, the name Menie is still recognized in Eastern Northumberland.

MINA. Little Mina has almost disappeared. This postal hamlet used to be in Hamilton Township, about half-way between the villages of Cold Springs and Johnstown. Like Penryn and Skibbereen (see below), the name "Mina" wasn't added to the landscape until the early 1900s, when Mina P.O. opened in 1904. The name can be traced to Mina Henderson, the daughter of a prominent early settler of Hamilton Township, Richard Henderson.

ONGLEY. From 1866 'til 1874, there was an obscure post office named Ongley on the 3rd Line of Brighton Township. The post office was in the area now called Carman (so called after the Carman Church) and run by settler P. H. Maybee. The name "Ongley" can be traced to a little four-corners village in Kent, England, though why the name was picked for the office isn't known.

ORLAND. Orland hamlet, near the intersection of Highway 30 and Northumberland Road 28, used to be a busy mill town in Brighton Township. Originally, the village was supposed to have been called "Dorland"—that was the name requested by the postmaster in 1898. (Previously, the community had been known as Newcomb's Mills.) The government turned him down because there was already a Dorland P.O. in Lennox & Addington County. So a post office bureaucrat simply knocked the "D" off "Dorland" and sent back a postal hammer marked "Orland!" Orland post office closed in 1941, and the mill is now an antique shop.

PENRYN & SHILOH. Between 1903 and 1912, the little hamlet of Shiloh in Cramahe Township went under the post office name Penryn. Penryn is no longer used, Shiloh again having become the official name of this community. The word *penryn* is actually from Cornish, a Celtic language (related to Welsh) which has been virtually extinct since the 1700s. In Cornish, a *penryn* is a promontory or hill, a good description of Shiloh's secluded location in the Northumberland hills. Penryn was chosen for the post office here apparently by or for several families of Cornish settlers here.

The name Shiloh—probably best known from the desperate Battle of Shiloh in the American Civil War—is biblical in origin. The original town of Shiloh is in Israel, about thirty kilometers north of Jerusalem. The town has long been an important religious centre, and many Christian churches have been named Shiloh to honor this community. In Hebrew, Shiloh means "the place of peace."

PERCY BOOM. This hamlet near the Seymour-Brighton border has one of the most unusual names in Eastern Ontario. The name has been in use on this part of the Trent River for well over a century, and now appears on the road leading from Highway 30 into the hamlet. The name came about because of the Trent-Severn Canal, which bypasses Percy Boom a short distance to the east. A detour was necessary because the river was extremely rough between Campbellford and Percy Reach. The rapids were so bad the government declared this section of the Trent unnavigable. However, timber was still floated down the river west of the canal, and to control the movement of the logs a floating barrier—a "boom"—was built across the mouth of Percy Reach. The log drivers (several of whom lost their lives on this part of the Trent) could move the logs in large, controlled rafts in and out of Percy Reach, preventing log-jams upstream. There hasn't been a log drive on the Trent for years, and the boom that gave Percy Boom its name has been dismantled. The hamlet is now packed with summer cottages.

RED CLOUD. Red Cloud hamlet is tucked in the northwestern corner of Cramahe Township, down the Red Cloud School Road. The Red Cloud School was S.S. #24 of Cramahe, and until very recently the school building was still standing beside the Red Cloud Cemetery. The village grew up around a mill on Dawson Creek, and the community was often referred to as simply Dawson Creek. The origin of Red Cloud has mystified local residents . . . a freighter that sank off Prince Edward County was called the Red Cloud, though the ship was probably built long after the community was named.

There is a village called Red Cloud in Nebraska, though there's no conclusive evidence to show this name migrated to Northumberland from the Mid-west. It's more than coincidence, however, that there are villages near the Nebraska Red Cloud called Hastings, Naponee, Minden, Kearney, Stella, and Odessa, all community names from Eastern Ontario. In the latter half of the 19th century, tens of thousands of farmers left Ontario for the Mid-west—not only were Ontario place-names taken to the States by these settlers, Canadians learned about American place-names through their ex-patriot relatives. The inspiration of "Red Cloud" was probably as simple as a Nebraska sunset, though it may have some connection to the First Nations People. The famous American novelist, Willa Cather, hailed from Red Cloud, Nebraska, so perhaps a Cather fan named the Canadian community.

SHELTER VALLEY. You can see this scenic valley from the 401, which crosses Shelter Valley Road just east of Grafton. The inspiration for the name is obvious—the valley is one of the deepest in the county, with steep, forested hills. Farms along the road are extremely well protected from bad weather. Shelter Valley Creek runs along the valley floor for almost ten kilometres, ending the hills near the Alderville Reserve.

SHILOH. See Penryn.

SKIBBEREEN. The unique name of Skibbereen briefly appeared on a post office in Haldimand Township. For about a decade after the turn of the century, Skibbereen P.O. served farmers around what is now the intersection of Highway 45 and County Road 22. There are two possible origins for the name, both of which are equally plausible. There is a village in Ireland's County Cork known as Skibbereen, and there were many settlers from Cork in Eastern Ontario. However, there is also a village in Durham, England, known as Skibbereen— the Canadian Durham County lies immediately adjacent to our Northumberland, within a few kilometres of Skibbereen. The Irish Skibbereen may be the original, as the first settlers in the district were the Irish O'Brien family. It's unfortunate this distinctive place-name no longer appears on maps of Northumberland, as Skibbereen P.O. was renamed "Mill Valley" in 1911. In Irish Gaelic, Skibbereen is written *an Sciobairín* and means "the place of small ships."

STONEY LONESOME. The name Stoney Lonesome appears on a dirt road running southwest of Morganston in Cramahe Township. The origin of the distinctive name isn't known for certain—at least one source connects it to some kind of Scottish literary reference, though that reference hasn't come to light. "Stoney Lonesome" might be just descriptive, as in the American Mid-west a patch of poor soil was often referred to as a stoney lonesome. (The soil here is certainly stony enough to warrant the name!) The presence of nearby Red Cloud (see above), a name which also from the American Mid-west, seems to back up this theory.

TWELVE O'CLOCK POINT. Twelve O'Clock Point is at the eastern entrance to the Murray Canal, just south of Trenton on Highway 33. With the exception of aboriginal names like Ganaraska, Twelve O'Clock Point is probably the oldest place-name still in use in Northumberland County. This point features in a story about French explorer Samuel de Champlain, one of the first Europeans to investigate the Lake Ontario shore line. During one of his trips through this area, de Champlain and his men traveled up the Bay of Quinte, the angular bay separating Prince Edward County from Hastings. De Champlain's party reached the head of the bay—then dominated by a large marsh and winding Dead Creek—and stopped to eat at noon. Since then, the point of land where they stopped has been called Twelve O'Clock Point.

WOOLER. This village in Murray Township sounds like it might have something to do with sheep farming, but its name really comes from a milling town in England's Northumberland. The original Wooler is found northwest of Alnwick, which probably accounts for its presence here—our Northumberland's smallest township is also called Alnwick. The English town was also the site of a battle won by the Percy family, who are remembered in Northumberland's Percy Township. In Old English, the word "wooler" (a contraction of *wella* and *ofer*) means "the mill on the spring," and the Canadian town featured a mill on a small creek.

16. Peterborough County

The Kawartha Lakes and the Trent-Severn Canal divide sprawling Peterborough County into two distinct halves. The southern part of the county is home to the city of Peterborough, an important regional centre and home to most of the county's population. The Kawarthas are a very popular tourist destination, and the population along the lakes doubles or triples in the summer months. In contrast, northern Peterborough is deep in the Canadian Shield, with hundreds of lakes and a few isolated villages. In both the north and the south, the early settlers were mostly Irish, and Irish names can be found among the communities. Many First Nations people still inhabit the Kawartha Lakes, and aboriginal names are common in the northern parts of Peterborough. The county was named for the city, established in the 1820s by Upper Canadian politician Peter Robinson. The English city of Peterborough may have inspired the final form of the name.

APSLEY. Apsley is a bustling village at the intersection of four different highways (28, 504, 620, and A620) in Anstruther Township. The village was always an important stopover on the old Burleigh Colonization Road, and is still the main centre for northeastern Peterborough. The community was apparently named by the Vizard family for the Barony of Apsley, a title of the Bathurst family in England. The Bathursts were relatives of the Duke of Richmond, an early and well loved governor of Upper Canada. One Baron Apsley was a prominent politician when Apsley Post Office was named, and may have inspired the choice. He was said to be the last man in London to wear a pigtail (definitely out of fashion in the mid-1800s), and when he finally relented and cut it off, he sent it around to his colleagues in a government envelope! The Bathursts' home, Apsley House in Sussex, was later sold to the renowned Duke of Wellington—his residence at Apsley may also have inspired the name for Apsley P.O. There's even an old story about a black sheep of the Bathurst family living in or near Apsley, but no documentary evidence about this person has appeared.

ASPHODEL. The name of this township is properly said "ASH-fo-del," even though it looks like "AHS-fo-del." Since 1821, this marshy stretch of the Trent River has traveled under the name Asphodel, which comes from ancient Greek. A half-dozen species of European lily, including the King's Spear and the Scotch Asphodel, are part of the genus *asphodel*. (In English, the word was originally translated as "affodil," which led to the name "daffodil" for those popular Easter-time flowers.) Tramping through the Trent River marshes, the surveyor may have been inspired to name the township "Asphodel" from the water lilies he saw around him.

BOSCHINK. The meaning of this Ojibwa word, properly said "BOW-shink," is not hard to guess if you know its location. The name was applied to a very narrow part of Stony Lake, and in Ojibwa "Boschink" is "the narrowing of the waters." Boschink Narrows was long graced by the popular Glenwood hotel, which—from 1915 to 1916—was home to Boschink Post Office.

BUCKHORN. There aren't many place-names in Eastern Ontario that can evoke the image of the bush country like Buckhorn. This Kawartha hamlet, at the head of Buckhorn Lake in Harvey Township, went by the more pedestrian name "Hall's Bridge" until World War II. John Hall was the community's first settler, and when a post office was granted in 1860, it was named for the pioneering Irishman. In 1941, local residents opted to rename the village Buckhorn after Buckhorn Lake—that name had been in use as far back as the 1840s. "Buckhorn" was probably inspired by the good deer hunting to be found in Harvey Township, though another story credits John Hall's collection of buck antlers as the source of Buckhorn.

CATCHACOMA. This isolated hamlet is in the heart of Cavendish Township. Pronounced just as it's written, Catchacoma is an aboriginal name possibly taken from the Ojibwa language. The word means simply "big water," and the village is located on Catchacoma Lake, one of Peterborough's larger bodies of water. The lake's name has also been written as "Catchicommu," though Catchacoma is now the only approved spelling. Until 1902, Catchacoma village was called Stratton after a local settler.

CHANDOS. The Township of Chandos is at the northeastern corner of Peterborough County. This oddly shaped township has a Scottish bent to its village names (see both Glen Aldaand Lasswade, below), but "Chandos" itself is connected to a powerful Englishman. William Wyndham Grenville (see Grenville County), the Duke of Buckingham and Britain's prime minister from 1806 to 1807, had among his multitudinous titles "the Duke of Chandos." The title Baron, and later Duke, of Chandos was created for the wealthy Chandos family of England. Their surname can be traced back to a Norman knight, Sir John Chandos, who hailed from the French town of Candos. Over the centuries, the "C" was corrupted into a "Ch" by the English. The township's name has also been credited to a member of the Chandos family—he was said to have lived in Peterborough County during the 1850s or 1860s.

CHEMONG. The aboriginal name "Chemong" (or "Chemung") has been applied, officially or unofficially, to several lakes around Eastern Ontario. Peterborough's Chemong is found in Smith Township, where the community now called Curve Lake was known as "Chemong P.O." from 1899 to 1904. Curiously, the long, curving lake by Curve Lake village isn't called Curve Lake, but Chemong Lake. Thomas Need, the founder of Bobcaygeon (see Victoria County), says Chemong was a name used in the 1830s when he first arrived in Peterborough. The meaning assigned to the word "chemong" is "lake of canoes," and it is pronounced "SHUH-mawng" or "SHUH-mung."

CLANRICARDE. It is very surprising this Irish name appears in a very Irish county like Peterborough, as the progenitor of the Clanricarde name was despised in Ireland. Hubert de Burgh-Canning, the Marquis of Clanricarde and Baron Somerhill, was a 19th century Irish noble and a one-time British diplomat. He became notorious in Ireland as an oppressive, tyrannical land baron, who treated his peasant farmers like cattle. Clanricarde's rule was so hated it led to an armed rebellion in Western Ireland in the late 19th century. Even arch-conservative British MPs thought Clanricarde was too conservative for them. His name was given to this post office in Burleigh Township in 1882, before his credibility was permanently destroyed by the armed riots. Most of Clanricarde's property was in County Galway, which probably accounts for his name appearing near Peterborough's own Galway Township. The accent falls on the last syllable of Clanricarde's name ("clan-ruh-CARD").

CLARINA. Like Clanricarde, Clarina owes its origin to an Irish peer. Baron Clarina was the title of the Massey family, whose many members owned land in several Irish counties. They took their title from a small Limerick town, whose name probably means "a little plain or clearing" in Irish Gaelic. The impressively named Eyre Challoner Henry Massey, the 4th Baron Clarina, was a decorated military officer and descendant of an Irish commander in the Seven Years' War. The name Clarina was chosen for this Dummer Township post office in 1898—the office closed in 1969, and the name no longer sees much use. Officially, the community is at the intersection of Peterborough Roads 6 and 40. The village of Routhier in Prescott County was also known as "Clarina" for a time.

COTTESLOE. Cottesloe village is in Dummer Township, at the junction of County Road 8 and the 4th Line. The community's name is linked to an Irish nobleman, Thomas Fremantle, Baron Cottesloe. Fremantle was a British MP and cabinet minister, holding ministerial responsibility for Ireland at one time. His father had served with Nelson at the Battle of Trafalgar. Our Cottesloe Post Office was named in 1886, shortly before Fremantle's death in 1890.

DOURO. The Township of Douro is on the southeast side of the Otonabee River, taking in a large swampy area near Peterborough city. As with Chandos (see above), Douro takes its name from a title of Arthur Wellesley, the Duke of Wellington. After winning a major battle along Portugal's Douro River, Wellington was created "Baron Douro" by the English government. The township was named in 1821, a few years after this title had been conferred, and a local post office was also named simply Douro in 1890. (Previously it had been called "South Douro," because Lakefield village went by "North Douro" until 1875.) The name is correctly pronounced "DOO-row," not like the word "dour."

DUMMER. Dummer Township is located on the Trent-Severn, split by the Indian River and separated from Burleigh Township by Stony Lake. The township remembers a Canadian judge of the early 19th century, William Dummer Powell. Powell was the chief justice of Upper Canada around the beginning of the 1800s. He later served as a cabinet minister and speaker of the Upper Canadian assembly. Curiously, Dummer's name has also ended up on a small village in Saskatchewan.

KASSHABOG LAKE. This large, comma-shaped lake is right at the centre of Methuen Township. Until recently, the MacDonald Bay summer post office was on a peninsula at the lake's north end. The name *Kasshabog* is an aboriginal word, which is said to mean "long and narrow waters"—a good description of the lake's shape. From 1959 to 1969, there was also a Kasshabog Post Office in Methuen.

LASSWADE. Lasswade hamlet is at the intersection of Highway 504 and Peterborough Road 46 in Chandos Township. The hamlet's name comes from a small town in Scotland—the original Lasswade is in Lothian Region. The name has two possible meanings, one Gaelic ("the fort in the thicket," *lios bhaid)* and the other Old English ("the fjord of the meadow," *laes gewaed*).

MISQUAA ZIIBI. This Ojibwa name, meaning "the red river," is the most recent addition to the Peterborough landscape. In early 1994, the Ontario Geographic Names Board agreed to restore Misquaa Ziibi in place of Squaw River. (The river runs from near Mississauga Lake through Harvey Township into the Kawarthas.) The river was called "Squaw" by the European settlers— they heard the element "squaw" in Misquaa Ziibi, and associated that element with the word squaw, a derogatory term for an aboriginal woman. The Anishnabe people of the Curve Lake First Nation asked to have this offensive name dropped. Misquaa Ziibi is only one example of an old aboriginal name being resurrected or redefined (see Mississagagon Lake under Frontenac County).

NEPHTON. This village is at the end of Peterborough Road 6, just over the western border of Methuen Township. Like many communities in this region, Nephton grew up around a mine, in this case a nepheline operation. (Nepheline is a metallic ore used in manufacturing ceramics.) As a place-name, Nephton is a newcomer to Methuen, the community having received its official name and post office only in 1961.

NOGIES CREEK. Nogies Creek (which, despite the temptation, is pronounced "NOHG-ees," not "NUG-ees!") is at the mouth of its namesake creek in Harvey Township. The name is misleading, because it's really in the possessive—Peter Nogy (or Nogie) was a Mississauga leader who lived in Harvey Township during European settlement. Nogy was a friend and ally of the settlers, and his name became attached to the creek where he once trapped. Later, in 1905, the post office was named after the creek. Just southeast of Furnace Falls (see Haliburton County) there is also a "Nogies Lake," named for the same man.

SERPENT MOUNDS. This somewhat eerie name was given to a provincial park on the north shore of Rice Lake. Serpent Mounds describes a series of long, serpentine burial mounds, used by the ancestors of the First Nations People at the nearby Hiawatha Reserve. At one time, these mounds were excavated and the contents on display to the public—out of respect to the people at Hiawatha, the mounds have now been returned to their original state. The park is just south of Keene village on Peterborough Road 34.

VIAMEDE. Viamede is occasionally shown in Burleigh Township, about half-way between Burleigh Falls and Mount Julian. There isn't much of a community to speak of there—the name really comes from the Viamede Hotel, which has been in business for most of this century. In Latin, "via mede" means "by way of the middle," referring to the approach visitors had to take to get to the Viamede. Sailing along Stony Lake, you had to cross the centre of the lake near Juniper Island to land at the hotel.

WARSAW. The name of the capital of Poland has found its way to a village near the Dummer-Douro townline. Unlike Wilno (see Renfrew County), the choice of the name wasn't made by Polish settlers in Peterborough County. Thomas Choate, a well-known businessman and the village's first postmaster, picked Warsaw because he had worked as an apprentice millwright in Warsaw, New York. The name has been in continuous use here since 1841.

17. Haliburton County

Haliburton County is a vast stretch of the Canadian Shield, at the outer limits of what's considered Eastern Ontario. Despite its geographic extent (twenty-four townships covering 4 500 km$^{2)}$ there are only 11 000 people here, giving Haliburton the smallest population of any county or district in Ontario. The place-names here often have cheeky anecdotes behind them, or are oddly mismatched (like the series of Welsh township names where hardly a Welsh soul could be found), assigned by government officials to bush country they probably never saw. The stories would have been appreciated by the county's namesake, T. C. Haliburton, a popular Canadian author who invented the immortal character Sam Slick. Haliburton's satirical and humorous books were known internationally in the 1800s, and he had recently died when the Ontario government decided to name this rugged county for him in 1874.

ALLSAW. Allsaw hamlet is in Minden Township, on the shores of the tongue-twisting Lake Kashagawigamog (see below). Like many other communities in Haliburton, Allsaw grew up around a sawmill. The name has an obvious inspiration: when the village met to decide on a new post office name in 1885, one lumberjack suggested "Allsaw" because it was "all sawing" in this tiny lumber town. The people agreed. Allsaw P.O. was open for business until 1942, when much of the sawing in southern Haliburton had stopped for lack of local sawlogs.

AUNT SARAH'S LOOKOUT. One of the best-loved names in Haliburton is Aunt Sarah's Lookout, found on the shore of Halls Lake in Stanhope Township. The little headland was named after an elderly member of the Welch family, who enjoyed watching the sunset from this spot. Aunt Sarah's Lookout has no official standing as a place-name, but is still remembered long after Sarah Welch has passed away.

BICROFT. At barely thirty kilometers^2, Bicroft is almost Ontario's smallest township. The little T-shaped municipality was split off from surrounding Cardiff Township when a uranium mine opened near Cardiff village. The village was given its own municipal government through the township, which has now outlasted the mine. "Bicroft" was invented by the mining company that moved into town, probably based on the name of nearby Bancroft.

BOSKUNG. This name, which is often spelled "Boshkung," was applied to a Stanhope Township post office from 1878 until 1963. There is still a Boshkung Lake in the vicinity of the old office, northwest of Carnarvon village. The word "boshkung" is definitely aboriginal in origin, but its meaning is disputed. Some sources translate "boshkung" as the "meeting of the waters," while others give the meaning as "three waters"—it's not clear what lakes or rivers are meant by "three waters."

DEVIL'S CREEK / IRONDALE. The hamlet of Irondale, in the eastern part of Snowdon, was long a key centre in Haliburton's mining industry. Major deposits of iron were found here, and it's likely that both "Devil's Creek" and "Irondale" were inspired by the presence of iron. Places associated with iron mining sometimes have "Devil" names for obvious reasons (i.e., hell, burning forges, etc.!) What was known as Devil's Creek is also a tortured stretch of water, devilishly difficult to drive logs through, I'm sure. The community was called "Devil's Creek P.O." from 1874 to 1883, and has been the more straightforward "Irondale" since then.

ELEPHANT LAKE. Elephants are pretty scarce in Haliburton County, but nevertheless there is an Elephant Lake in the Township of Harcourt. The name was given because of the lake's shape — Elephant Lake looks remarkably like the head of an elephant in profile. There's even an island to mark where the eye would be.

EYRE. Eyre Township is one component of the huge municipality called Dysart, Bruton, Clyde, Dudley, Eyre, Guilford, Harburn, Harcourt & Havelock. (Frequently the township is shortened to Dysart et al, the other eight townships being dubbed "the et als" as a result.) Located in the central part of Haliburton, Eyre was surveyed and named in 1872. The "Eyre" is General Sir William Eyre, who briefly served as acting governor-general (officially titled the administrator) in 1857. While Governor Sir Edmund Head was away in England, Eyre filled in. The name is usually pronounced like the word "air."

FURNACE FALLS. This village is on Highway 503, near the boundary of Snowdon and Galway Townships. The name Furnace Falls is probably a play on words: while there were furnaces in the area, serving the district's mines, the village's founder—Richard Carr—was from Barrow-in-Furness in England. This "Furness" has nothing to do with mines, but is a rugged peninsula on England's Irish Sea coast. Richard Carr's family ran the Furnace Falls Post Office from 1911 until it was abolished in 1967, and descendants of Carr still live in and around Furnace Falls. (See also Furnace Falls under Leeds County.)

GELERT. The hamlet of Gelert in Snowdon Township takes its name from an enduring Welsh legend. In the Dark Ages, the Welsh Prince Llewellyn was given a greyhound named Gelert by England's King John. When Llewellyn went on a hunting trip, he left Gelert to guard his infant son in his crib. The prince returned home to discover his son's crib empty and Gelert covered in blood. Enraged, Llewellyn slew the dog, thinking it had eaten his son. He soon discovered, however, that Gelert had saved the child from a hungry wolf, and it was the wolf's blood on the dog's fur. The repentant prince had Gelert buried in a special tomb, which is said to be in the Welsh town now called Beddgelert ("Gelert's Grave" in Welsh). Many historians now believe the story of the dog is a myth, but the name Gelert lives in both in Wales and in Haliburton. Appropriately, our Gelert is in Snowdon Township—Gelert's grave is in the Snowdonia hills of northwestern Wales. "Gelert" was approved for the local post office in 1879.

GOODERHAM. With the exception of Corbyville (see Hastings County), Gooderham is the only community in Eastern Ontario named for a brewery. In 1873, a travelling salesman from Toronto's Gooderham Distilleries arrived in the village (then called Pine Lake), and gave the local tavern several kegs of whiskey as a promotion. Pine Lake's residents enjoyed a major bash on the free booze that night. The morning after, and feeling grateful under the influence, the residents of Pine Lake resolved to rename their town Gooderham. The name was approved for the post office in 1873, and is still here, even though Gooderham Distilleries is history.

HOTSPUR. Tiny Hotspur is just off Highway 503 in Monmouth Township. The intriguing name was assigned to a post office here from 1879 to 1923, and is still heard in Haliburton today. The source of the Hotspur name is a warlike member of the Percy family, one of the hereditary earls of Northumberland. This particular earl earned the nickname "Hotspur" from his hot temper and bloodthirsty nature.

IRONDALE. See Devil's Creek.

IRONSIDES & RADIUM SPRINGS. The name of Ironsides hamlet evokes images of the railway era, and that's probably where the name "Ironsides" came from. Steam trains were often called "iron horses" in the 19th century—when a railway line was built through the eastern townships of Haliburton, the name "Ironsides" probably seemed appropriate for a community in this area. Ironsides was also called Radium Springs for a mineral spring located near town. The hamlet is now located on what's called the Loop, a series of villages in Monmouth, Harcourt, and Cardiff Townships all connected by Highway 648. Ironsides, which never had a post office, is in the northwestern corner of Cardiff.

KENNISIS LAKE. This popular vacation spot is in the central Haliburton township of Havelock. The name, which is pronounced "kin-EE-sus," was given to a summer post office here in 1962. (Like most other summer offices, Kennisis Lake P.O. was closed recently.) The unusual name remembers an aboriginal man, Joe Kennisis, who lived and trapped near the lake. His family lived here for five generations before the first European settlement.

KILCOO CAMP. Another of Haliburton's many holiday spots is Kilcoo Camp, located on the east shore of Gull Lake in Lutterworth Township. A summer post office called "Kilcoo Camp" opened here in 1953, and probably saw thousands of postcards home before it closed in 1978. Despite its recent arrival in Haliburton, the name "Kilcoo" has ancient origins in County Down, Ireland. A village in Down is called Kilcoo because of its venerable church—in Gaelic, the name means "the Church of Cua."

LAKE KASHAGAWIGAMOG. This classic Haliburton place-name in found on a narrow lake running southwest of Haliburton village. There seem to be several competing pronunciations (not surprisingly)—two of the more common are "kah-SHAY-guh-wig-uh-mawg" and "KASH-uh-gug-wig-uh-mawg." The name is aboriginal in origin, meaning the "long and winding waters." If ever there was a name that suited its meaning, long and winding Lake Kashagawigamog is it!

LOCHLIN. Lochlin hamlet is in the northeastern part of Snowdon Township, a short drive from Haliburton village. The name was chosen for the village post office in 1895—the community was originally called Egypt, but another Egypt in southwestern Ontario forced a name change for this office. It's not clear what inspired the choice of Lochlin. The most obvious source, Snowdon's namesake region in Wales, doesn't have a place name anything like Lochlin. Several lakes in the British Isles have the same pronunciation ("LOCK-lin"), including Lough Leane in Ireland's County Kerry, and Loch Linne in Scotland. Lough Leane may be the inspiration, as Snowdon Township was dubbed "Little Ireland" from its large Irish population. Lochlin is also an alternative spelling of the name "Laughlin," so there may have been a Lochlin family somewhere in Snowdon.

OXTONGUE LAKE. This odd name is found in McClintock Township, where there is also an Oxtongue River and (until just recently) an Oxtongue Lake Post Office. Local tradition says that when the surveyor passed through McClintock, he decided to name this lake Oxtongue because it was shaped like an ox tongue. (I can't see it myself!) Oxtongue Lake P.O. was established in 1942. The river itself is now part of Oxtongue River Provincial Park.

PAUDASH LAKE. See Paudash under Hastings County.

RACKETY. Rackety hamlet is on Gull Lake, directly across from Kilcoo Camp (see above) in Lutterworth. The community never had a post office, so we have no official record of where the name might have come from. The best guess is that the name was taken from the sound of the logs in the slide — rackety would be perhaps the tamest description of the noise! The area around Rackety always had a thriving lumber industry, so it's possible to imagine the inspiration for the name.

RADIUM SPRINGS. See Ironsides.

TORY HILL. This village name in Monmouth Township often provokes the question, "Is this a Tory, as in a Conservative?" Much to the chagrin of one 19th century Liberal, this is precisely where the name came from. In 1893, when the village was asked to provide a name for its post office, a public meeting was called to discuss the issue. After several hours of fruitless debate, one local resident — well-known as the only Liberal supporter in town — joked that they should call the place "Tory Hill" because there were so many Conservatives in town. To his dismay, the local Tories took him up on the idea! It was doubly mortifying, as the Liberal lived right at the top of the hill overlooking town. The story of Tory Hill's name has become a local legend in Monmouth Township.

URSA. Ursa hamlet is on Glamorgan Township's 10th Line, a few kilometres east of Haliburton Road 3. An old post office name from the 1880s, Ursa was inspired by two constellations you can see on any clear Haliburton night—Ursa Major, the Great Bear, and Ursa Minor, the Little Bear, are visible year-round at the centre of the northern sky. Ursa P.O. closed in 1926, and the name has limited recognition in Haliburton today.

WILBERFORCE. The village of Wilberforce is on Highway 648, part of the Loop in the eastern Haliburton Highlands. Like Wilberforce Township in Renfrew County, the village was named for a famous anti-slavery crusader in England, William Wilberforce. Throughout his career as a member of the British Parliament, Wilberforce fought to have slavery abolished throughout the Empire. His battle finally succeeded in 1833, though he died before emancipation legislation could be enacted. This village was named Wilberforce in December of 1879, about thirty years after the Renfrew township.

18. The Old County of Durham

If you look at the road map of Ontario today, you'll find the "Regional Municipality of Durham" hugging the eastern border of Metropolitan Toronto. This, however, is not the Durham many Ontario residents will remember—until the 1970s, Durham was a small, square county occupying the space between Northumberland, Peterborough, Victoria, and what was called Ontario County. When regional government came to town, old Durham was split up: Hope Township went to Northumberland, Cavan Township to Peterborough, Manvers Township to Victoria, and the Townships of Clarke, Darlington, and Cartwright became the eastern part of the new Durham Region. (Those three also lost their individual existence, as Clarke and Darlington were merged into the Town of Newcastle, and Cartwright into the Township of "Scugog.") For most of its lifetime, Durham was united with Northumberland for municipal purposes, and so it's fitting that the true County of Durham be included in this book. We shouldn't be surprised to find the name "Durham" here—the English Durham County is the southern neighbor of the English Northumberland. (In Old English, Durham means "the island with the hill.")

ANTIOCH. SS #8 of Clarke Township was long known as the "Antioch School." This area seems to have a curious attachment to middle eastern names (see Cairo, below), of which Antioch is another example. The city of Antioch was a key centre during the Crusades of the Middle Ages—European invaders made Antioch a base of operations for their war. Clarke's Antioch school (also known as Gamsby's School for the local Gamsby family) was established early on in township history, probably before 1840.

CADMUS. This Cartwright Township village takes its name from the ancient Greek Cadmus, credited with creating the Greek alphabet. The choice was made by settler John Hughes, who suggested "Cadmus" to the village's first postmaster, George Workman, in 1871. Cadmus is now part of the restructured Township of Scugog.

CAESAREA. If you asked for directions to Caesarea, a bustling village in Cartwright Township, you'd probably get a blank look unless you said you were looking for "siz-uh-REE-uh!" The quirky pronunciation belies the name's obvious origin—the Caesar family were leading citizens of the area, and in 1853 they were honored in the postal name. Being located on Lake Scugog, Caesarea always had strong "maritime" ties to the shipping industry.

CAIRO. The name "Cairo" has a long, but murky, relationship with Durham County. There may have been a Cairo in either Cavan or Manvers Townships as far back as 1835—Floreen Carter reports she found an ancient note in the post office files instructing that mail bound for "Cairo Post Office" should be routed via Cavan. The only problem is there's nothing else to indicate there ever was a Cairo P.O.

However, the name crops up again in a second story relating to Cavan Township. School Section #9 of Cavan was named "Cairo" at the suggestion of a local farmer. He remembered that early in the 1800s, there was one year when Cavan was the only township in the area where the wheat crop hadn't failed miserably. People were travelling for dozens of miles to get seed from Cavan farmers, so many people that it was compared to an ancient (Biblical, perhaps?) mass migration to Egypt. The 9th line of Cavan became known as the Egypt Road after this incident. When the school section was created on the 9th line, this farmer recalled the Egypt Road story and suggested Cairo for the school. It seems likely there could be a simpler explanation—somewhere in the dim and misty, there was a short-lived Cairo Post Office in northern Cavan, and the name was passed down orally until it reached the Cairo school. The post office may have also inspired, or could have been inspired by, the "Egypt" story.

CAVAN. Like many other places in the Peterborough area, Cavan's name is taken directly from Ireland. Cavan is the name of both a county on the border of Northern Ireland and the chief town of the same county. Cavan is translated closely from the Gaelic phrase *an Cabhá,* which means "the hollow." The name is apt for both locations, as both are in rolling, hilly territory. Our Cavan Township was named in 1816, and a local village has gone by the postal name Cavan since 1830. Appropriately, the Townships of North and South Monaghan are Cavan's neighbors to the east, just as County Monaghan is the eastern neighbor of Ireland's County Cavan.

CHARLECOTE. You can't even find "Charlecote" on detailed maps of Hope Township today—the hamlet's location seems to have gone unrecorded. The name came into use in 1884, when farmer Thomas Purcell was appointed to run a new post office. He chose to call the office after the Warwickshire community of Charlecote, whose name has the curiously understated meaning "cottages of the freemen." (I expected something with more oomph from hard-bitten, independent warriors of the Middle Ages!) Charlecote P.O. closed in 1912 and seemingly took the name Charlecote with it.

COURTICE. "CUR-tis," as it's said in Darlington Township, is at the intersection of Highway 2 and Durham Road 34. Like Caesarea (see above), Courtice takes its name from a prominent local family—William and Charles Courtice once owned most of the land on which the village now stands. Courtice was still the postal address here until 1963.

DRANOEL STATION. The whistle-stop of Dranoel Station was located on the Canadian Pacific Railway line in Cavan Township. The name Dranoel Station, which is rarely heard in Cavan today, was the creation of a local railway official. When the line was being constructed, one of the railroad's chief executives (said to be a native of Bethany village in Manvers) was named Leonard. Asked to name for this rural station, the official suggested Dranoel, which was Leonard's name spelled backwards. Despite its odd spelling (I won't even make a guess at the pronunciation) Dranoel Station was approved.

GUIDE BOARD. See Welcome.

KELMAR. For a few years in the early part of this century, Kelmar P.O. served several rural families in the neighborhood of Frazerville. The office was in the home of one Robert Matchett, on the 7th Line of Cavan Township. Matchett concocted the name "Kelmar" from three local families: Kelly, Matchett, and Richardson. Kelmar closed in 1913, and residents were switched to R.R. 1 Frazerville.

LOTUS. The name of Lotus village in Manvers sounds like it might have some kind of oriental connection, like nearby Osaca (see below). However, the name is credited to the water lilies found in the marshy areas near Lotus. The village was originally known as "Frogpond," which gives further credence to this explanation. It is possible, though, that Lotus was named after a community in Scotland—for whatever reason, a town and a hill in Dumfries & Galloway Region are called "Lotus." There were a fair number of Scottish settlers in this part of Victoria, so it's possible someone could have known about Lotus, Scotland. Lotus P.O. was open from 1873 to 1914.

LOVEKIN. The area around Lovekin, in the front concessions of Clarke Township, is sparsely populated and quite isolated today. Back in the 1790s, however, this was the toe-hold of European settlement in Clarke Township. Richard Lovekin, an Irish settler from County Cork, landed here in 1795 to homestead on what's now called Graham's Creek. From there his family spread throughout Clarke, and the town of Newcastle eventually formed several kilometres northwest of his property. By the 1870s, there were no Lovekins left in the hamlet, though that has not prevented the name Lovekin from surviving until today.

OSACA. Osaca is still a busy hamlet on County Road 65, near the modern Northumberland-Durham border. The curious name has been given several possible origins, although the most obvious is that the village was named for Osaka, Japan. Japan was frequently in the news in the late 1860s and early 1870s, as the powerful emperor Meiji had just been crowned and begun a major wave of modernization. Part of that modernization was to open Japanese ports to European trade—Osaka was among the ports affected by this move.

However, it's also been suggested the name is an anagram of the expression "Old-Style Alexander Chopping Axe." It's possible (this version explains the spelling of Osaca with a "c") but I've never heard of an Old-Style Alexander Chopping Axe. Before Osaca Post Office opened in 1873, the village was known as Foxtown—the reason why has not been recorded.

PENIEL. A Biblical name, taken from Genesis 32:30, Peniel was originally just the name of a church in the 5th Concession of Hope. Later, the name became used for the surrounding hamlet, which is just southeast of Perrytown. The Biblical passage describes how, after a long pilgrimage and resettlement, the people decide to call their new home "Peniel." The name may have been given with the journey of Hope's European settlers in mind. Peniel is no longer a commonly used place-name.

PODONK CORNERS. The area around Lot 25, Concession 10 of Darlington Township has the good old rustic name of Podonk Corners. In the dialect of the New England states, a "podonk" is a small, rural, out-of-the-way place—this description fits our Podonk Corners perfectly. Apparently, the word Podonk is taken from one of the aboriginal languages of New England (Maliseet, maybe?) and is given the meaning "a swampy place." There are likely other Podonks (and podonks!) in Eastern Ontario, but this is the only one I've ever seen marked on a map.

PONTYPOOL. This village is near the southern border of Manvers Township, where Highway 35 meets Victoria Road 12. The community takes its name from a Welsh farming town in Gwent—in Welsh, "Pont-y-pool" means "the bridge (*pont*) by (*y*) the pool" (actually the English word, not a Welsh word). The name does *not* mean "the place of pools," as is often reported. The pool meant is probably the River Llwyd, which flows right through the Welsh town. Manvers' Pontypool was named by an early settler there, John Jennings, presumably when the post office opened in 1881. The name is occasionally spelt with an "e," Pontepool.

PORK HILL. This odd name appears on a hill in the 7th Concession of Hope Township. The pork in question was a wagon load of pigs, which, at some time in the dim and misty, overturned on this hill—the pigs escaped to freedom. Thereafter the spot was known as Pork Hill! The name is known locally but has no official sanction.

PURPLE HILL. From 1882 to 1913, the Purple Hill Post Office served several rural concessions in Cartwright Township. Apparently, the name was coined to reflect the view of this hilly country . . . in the haze of a summer sunset, the hills of Cartwright really do seem purple. Purple Hill is still a recognized place-name in the area.

QUAYS. Quays gives the impression it's on the waterfront, but the now-vanished hamlet is really inland in Hope's 4th Concession. Quays didn't exist until the Midland Railway was constructed—the last stop before Port Hope became known as Quays (or just Quay) Station, because a family of that name had been prominent settlers in the district. Thomas Quay and John Quay were both municipal officials in the 1820s. The railway disappeared decades ago, and for the most part the name Quays went with it. The hamlet had a post office from 1904 until 1914.

SCUGOG. This lake, which was created by damming in the early 19th century, forms the northwestern boundary of old Durham County. Pronounced "SKOO-gawg," the name is now used for a large municipality in Durham Region (see the introduction to this chapter), and for a long, narrow island in Scugog Lake. Before regional government was implemented in Durham, this island was the incorporated Township of Scugog. The name is definitely aboriginal in origin, coming from a Mississauga phrase meaning "shallow, muddy place" or "drowned land." The phrase was substantially shortened by Europeans in the area to just "Scugog."

SOLINA. Solina, on a Darlington Township sideroad near Farewell Creek, got its name thanks to an enterprising public-school student. When the village was asked to provide a name for its new post office, the local schoolteacher randomly picked six letters—"A-N-L-S-O-I"—and asked his students to come up with a name using those letters. One student handed in "S-O-L-I-N-A," which became the official choice in 1869.

STONY BATTER. This slightly comical road name from Hope Township has nothing to do with a failed recipe, but is drawn from a Gaelic road name in Dublin. In Gaelic, the word for "road" is *bóthair,* and when English invaders heard *bóthair,* it was picked up as "batter." Therefore, Stony Batter Road in Dublin literally means "stony road road." Famine Irish likely brought the name to Durham in the 19th Century.

WELCOME / GUIDE BOARD. Welcome hamlet is a busy crossroads about five kilometers northwest of Port Hope, and one kilometer north of the 401. The village was also known as Guide Board in the early 1800s, and the names Guide Board and Welcome can both be traced to a road sign that once stood in the village. At the southwest corner of town, a large, multi-armed sign used to give directions and distances to communities in Hope Township. It's been suggested the word "Welcome" appeared at the top of the sign—as though it were the actual name of the community—and the hamlet subsequently became known as Welcome. The sign itself was referred to as a "guide board," and the name Guide Board became a shorthand reference to the village. The sign is no longer standing, and the name Guide Board has fallen out of use. Appropriately, the name Welcome is now prominently displayed on a modern 401 "guide board" near Port Hope.

YELVERTON. Yelverton hamlet is on Highway 7A, close to where the highway intersects Janetville Creek. The hamlet is in rolling, scrubby, and swampy country, and there are not many inhabitants here today. The country greatly resembles the moorlands of Devonshire, England, where the name "Yelverton" originated. The community was originally known as Elfordtown (literally "elder tree ford") but the Devonshire accent turned the name into Yelverton by the 1850s. Our Yelverton went by the non-descript name "Newry" until 1871.

19. Victoria County

Named for the first Queen of Canada, Victoria County reaches from the prosperous farmland near Scugog Lake north into the Canadian Shield. Most of the settlers to Victoria came long after the Loyalist era, and the place-names of this county reflect a more diverse population. You can find Scottish, Irish, and English place names in the right areas, as well as some unlikely migrants from Africa and Asia. Victoria also shares the Trent-Severn Waterway with Peterborough, and the Kawartha Lakes are dotted with aboriginal names. It's probably a stretch to include Victoria in a book on Eastern Ontario, as the county is really more closely tied into Central Ontario. But Victoria's amazing variety of names (and the stories about them) was too tempting to pass up.

AROS. The hamlet of Aros is in Bexley Township, a little municipality hugging the indented shoreline of Balsam Lake. Aros Post Office opened a year before Confederation, and closed down in 1884 due to slow business. The first postmaster, Scotsman Charlie McInnis, named his office after his home on the Isle of Mull, now in Strathclyde Region. The River Aros connects a small inland loch with the Sound of Mull, and where the river meets the sound is the tiny hamlet of Glen Aros. The Aros of Victoria County is no longer shown on the maps.

BADDOW. This post office name was given to a crossroads hamlet in Somerville Township. The crossroads, close to the eastern shore of Balsam Lake, was first called Ead's Settlement for the local Ead family. One Joseph Ead became the community's first postmaster in 1875, and he selected the name Baddow for his office. Baddow is an old river name from Essex, England, that has fallen out of use. The river is now called the Chelmer, but previously it was known as "the battle river" (*baddow* in Old English) though the "battle" fought there is not recorded. The Ead family traced its roots to Essex, and knew the Baddow name from there. The Canadian village is situated near a small river of its own, Corben Creek.

BOBCAYGEON. This attractive town is right in the heart of the Kawarthas, on the junction of Pigeon Lake and Sturgeon Lake. Founded by Englishman Thomas Need (a story recounted in his entertaining book *Six Years in the Bush*), Bobcaygeon was originally a mill town, but has now become a major tourist destination on the Trent-Severn. The village's name, pronounced "bawb-KAY-jun," sounds a bit like an exotic shrimp dish you might find in New Orléans. In fact, the unusual name was coined the aboriginal inhabitants of the area—in Mississauga, "bobcaygeon" means "the shallow rapids," referring to the rapids that once powered the village's sawmill. Need writes the community was first called Rokeby by Governor Sir John Colborne, but Bobcaygeon has been the official choice since the post office opened in 1853.

BOLSOVER. The Eldon Township village of Bolsover is one of many communities in Victoria with a transplanted English place-name. There are two Bolsovers in England's Derbyshire—a village of Bolsover, and a flatland called Bolsover Moor. The name goes back to Old English, in which the phrase "bolsover" means "the ridge of a man named Boll." Initially the Canadian village was called "Onnacome," but the post office name "Bolsover" eventually became the local preference. The office was named in 1864.

BURNT RIVER. Burnt River hamlet is near the centre of Somerville Township, just east of Four Mile Lake. Burnt River is one of the older place-names in Victoria—the actual river, which runs southwest across Somerville Township, was named some years before the village of Burnt River was settled. The source of "Burnt River" is said to be a huge forest fire that swept Somerville Township in the mid-1800s. Once the fire had passed, the story goes, the river was left a peculiar "burnt" color, perhaps from all the ash swept into the water. An alternative explanation is given by historian Gladys Suggitt, who wrote: "Burnt River is noted for the dark color of the water which flows beneath its banks, and which is caused by the mineral deposits picked up from the area through which it flows." This mineral is likely iron oxide.

The community now known as Burnt River was first called Rettie's Bridge, and (after the railway went through) Rettie's Station for a local family. The first postmaster wanted to rename Rettie's Station "Burnt River," but the village of Kinmount (see below) was already called Burnt River Crossing. The problem was solved by changing Burnt River Crossing to Kinmount. Burnt River Post Office then opened on Somerville's 7th Line in 1873.

THE CITY OF PEACE. The village of Victoria Road in Bexley Township was also known as "the City of Peace." It's been suggested the name was given tongue-in-cheek because Victoria Road was split between four different townships—Carden on the southwest, Dalton on the northwest, Digby on the northeast, and Laxton on the southwest. The residents, therefore, had to deal with at least three different township councils (Laxton and Digby having a joint council with Longford). This many competing bureaucrats and politicians mustn't have made for very much peace! The official name of Victoria Road is still in use today.

COBOCONK. For anyone writing about the place names of Eastern Ontario, Coboconk is an irresistible choice. The village is on the Bexley-Somerville boundary, along the broad Gull River. The Gull has a direct link to the word "coboconk"—despite its unusual look, the word is simply a shortened version of an aboriginal expression for "where the gulls nest." The name has been in use since 1859, when Coboconk P.O. was opened here. The office was briefly renamed Shedden between 1874 and 1880, but Coboconk has been in continuous use since then. The name is pronounced as it's written, "CO-buh-cawnk."

DONGOLA. Dongola hamlet is on Highway 503, between Kinmount and Norland. The community has dwindled since its peak at the turn of the century —the little school has closed, and the post office (once run from a local settler's kitchen) packed up in 1936. The curious name "Dongola" comes from a city in the African nation of the Sudan. During the latter part of the 19th century, the British made a major military campaign throughout Eastern Africa. (The hamlet of Khartum [see Renfrew County] also took its name from this campaign.) One of the major battles took place at Dongola, Sudan, and this Somerville Township hamlet may have commemorated the battle by naming itself "Dongola." Alternatively, the name may have been assigned by the Post Office Department.

FEIR'S MILL. The hamlet of Feir's Mill has dwindled to just a family or two in Ops Township. The community traces its name back to Alexander and Jane Feir, who arrived here in 1854 to settle a lot in the 10th Concession. The Feirs were Irish—they escaped the Famine, crossing the Atlantic and landing in Port Hope down on the lake. The Feirs built a mill near the source of Fleetwood and Pigeon Creeks, and though their operation was overshadowed by mills in Omemee, the name "Feir's Mill" continues to survive here.

FINGERBOARD. This bizarre post office name is still remembered in Mariposa Township, where Fingerboard P.O. was open from 1881 to 1913. The community was first known as "Port Hoover," but in 1881 the name was changed in honor of a local landmark. Right in town, there was a directional sign post shaped like a hand with a pointing finger—literally, a "finger board." The sign may have pointed the way to Port Perry, though there are conflicting stories. The name has been recorded as one word and as two ("Finger Board P.O.") An intersection in Frontenac County's Pittsburgh Township may also have been called Fingerboard, though there is no such place there now.

GLENARM / HARDSCRABBLE. The village of Glenarm is part of Eldon Township in central Victoria. This part of Eldon was settled largely by Scottish immigrants, and Glenarm is one of many place-names the Scots brought to Victoria. The original community of Glenarm is located in Scotland's Tayside Region. Even while the community's official postal name was Glenarm (from 1865 to 1968), many residents of Eldon knew this area by the colorful name Hardscrabble. The description "hardscrabble" may be new to city folk, but anyone who's farmed the less-than-choice soil of Eastern Ontario will know the word well. Marginal farms on poor soil are often dubbed "hardscrabble farms," and a goodly number of such farms in Eldon probably inspired the name.

HARDSCRABBLE. See Glenarm.

HELL'S HALF ACRE. This colorful name was applied to the hamlet of Corson's Siding in Bexley Township. The Siding had a reputation for being a rough and rowdy town with no shortage of booze. During the winter, writes Watson Kirkconnell, one Corson would bring in hired hands from the lakeshore townships to cut cordwood. These workers would then go out and get "half cut" themselves, the story goes. While the Hell's Half Acre description might refer to the hamlet's isolated location, the phrase may have been the invention of the ever-vigilant temperance forces.

ISLAY. Islay is another predominantly Scottish hamlet in western Victoria. (See also Glenarm, above, and Rohallion, below.) The area along the Eldon-Fenelon townline was settled by Scottish immigrants from the Island of Islay in Scotland. The name Islay isn't Gaelic, as might be expected, but Old Norse, meaning "the island of a man named Ile." Islay P.O. was granted in 1856. The presence of these Islay settlers also accounts for the name of nearby Argyle hamlet—Islay was formerly part of Argyllshire.

KINMOUNT. This hamlet is in northeastern Victoria, at the junction of four townships (Somerville, Galway, Snowdon, and Lutterworth) and three counties (Victoria, Peterborough, and Haliburton). Kinmount was originally a stopping place on the Bobcaygeon Settlement Road, which ran in a straight line from Bobcaygeon up to Minden village in Haliburton. Settlers arrived around 1860, and the isolated community was already an important service village for the surrounding townships by 1880. There are several explanations for the name Kinmount, given to the post office in 1859. A mansion in Dumfries and

Galloway Region, Scotland, is called Kinmount House, though there's no evidence any of the settlers here might have known about it. A second possible source is a poem of Sir Walter Scott's called "The Ballad of Kinmont Willie"— Scott's works were the inspiration for several other Eastern Ontario place-names. (For example, see Lammermoor under Lanark County and Ivanhoe under Hastings County.) A third suggestion, though somewhat far-fetched, is that the Scottish settlers in Somerville would say they "kin mount" the hills surrounding the village.

LITTLE BRITAIN. The name of this village in Mariposa evokes the old image of Ontarians being more British than the British. However, you may be surprised to learn the name really comes from the United States. Little Britain is a township in Lancaster County, Pennsylvania, named before the U.S. rebelled against British rule. That Little Britain, in turn, took its name from a district of London. The name "Little Britain" was assigned to our community's post office in 1855. Residents had originally supported the name "Elmgrove," but the incredible proliferation of names with "elm"—including Elmview, Elm Tree, Elmvale, Elm Brook, and just plain Elm in Eastern Ontario alone—forced the government to make another choice. Little Britain, like Dongola (see above) and Manilla (see below), may have been taken from a list of American place-names used by the government for naming new offices.

MANILLA. While Manila is definitely the capital of the Philippines, our Manilla seems to take its name from a village in Iowa. Of the half-dozen or so "Manilas" in the world, only ours and Iowa's spell their name with two "l"s. It's possible an American military action in the Philippines inspired the Iowa village's name—our Manilla probably came off the post office's stand-by list of American names. The name was approved in November, 1856, and in 1878 a second office called "Manilla Station" also opened in Mariposa Township.

MOUNT HOREB. This hamlet, which consists of only one or two houses now, is on the Ops-Manvers townline. Mount Horeb takes its name from a mountain in the Sinai region of Egypt—the mountain is mentioned in at least one passage in the Bible. Despite its tiny size, the community boasted a post office from 1863 until 1914. Mount Horeb is barely one kilometre away from Feir's Mill (see above).

OPS. Ops is one of the oldest townships in Victoria County, surrounding the county town of Lindsay. In ancient Roman mythology, Ops was the goddess of spring and of plenty, and her name was also the Latin word for "wealth." The name was given to this township in 1821 because of its good soil and agricultural potential.

ROHALLION. This Carden Township post office took its name from a Scottish castle in Perthshire (now Tayside Region). In Scottish Gaelic, the name is a corruption of a phrase meaning "the Fort of the Caledonians"—the inhabitants of Scotland, particularly of the outlying islands, were often called the Caledonians. "Caledonia" is an ancient and poetic name for Scotland used in many places around Ontario. (See Caledonia Flats under Prescott County, for example.) Rohallion P.O. was named in 1889.

SADOWA. The name of this hamlet near the northern edge of Victoria commemorates an obscure battle in Austria. In 1866, the Prussians defeated the army of Austria at Sadowa, Bohemia, and went on to ravage the Austrian Empire. While the original Sadowa is pronounced "sah-DOV-uh," our Sadowa is usually said with a "w," i.e., "sah-DOW-uh." The name was picked up for this hamlet in 1881, likely from an American Sadowa (see Little Britain).

UPNOR. The name of Upnor, found on a remote hamlet in Carden Township, sounds as if it might have been coined from the community's location (i.e., "up north.") The most likely source, however, is a small bay in Kent, England, called Upnor Reach. The Reach is part of the Medway River system, and—ironically —the name "Upnor" really *does* come from a phrase meaning "up north" in Old English! The Canadian Upnor was probably named by the post office department in 1865.

VALENTIA. The attractive name of Valentia hamlet, in Mariposa Township, was first used for a local post office in 1866. The name may come from a minor noble family in the U.K.—the Annesley family took as their hereditary title Viscount Valentia. During the early settlement of Mariposa, Arthur Annesley, the 11th Viscount Valentia, was an English politician. There's no obvious reason for the connection, though like Cottesloe and Clarina in Peterborough (see above), a post office bureaucrat may have simply pulled "Valentia" from a dusty old peerage book! It's also possible someone took the name from Ireland's Valentia Island, located just off the coast of County Kerry. (Valentia is an English name, the island being referred to as *Dairbhe* ["place of oaks"] in Gaelic.) Valentia's first postmaster, William Sharp, may have hailed from Kerry.

VERULAM. The Township of Verulam is in the central part of Victoria, split in two by one of the beautiful Kawartha Lakes. The town of Bobcaygeon (see above) was part of Verulam before the town was incorporated. The name "Verulam" was originally coined for a title of the Grimston family of England—the Grimstons owned property near the ancient Roman city of Verulamium, a short distance northwest of London. James Grimston, the first Earl of Verulam (1775-1845) is credited as having inspired the name of Verulam Township in 1823. Grimston was the brother-in-law of a British prime minister, the Earl of Liverpool.

20. Nipissing District

The Upper Madawaska

The District of Nipissing isn't really part of Eastern Ontario. The District's huge expanse—most of which is in Algonquin Provincial Park—is really part of the "Near North," the fuzzy overlap between the true "East" and the true "North" in Ontario. However, a tiny square of Nipissing is trapped south of Algonquin, separated from the rest of the District by hundreds of kilometres of bush. This parcel of five townships—Airy, Dickens, Lyell, Murchison, and Sabine, plus a small corner of Clancy Township—is often called the "Upper Madawaska," as the townships are in the northernmost reaches of the Madawaska River watershed. The communities of the Upper Madawaska have always looked to nearby Barrys Bay and Renfrew County for services, and as a result have a *de facto* link to Eastern Ontario. Lumber is still king in this isolated district, and some of the local place-names reflect this lumbering tradition. Nipissing itself is an aboriginal name, probably Algonquin in origin, meaning "the little body of water"—the word refers to Lake Nipissing near present-day North Bay.

AIRY. This township of eight hundred people is bounded by Algonquin on two sides, and is frequently nicknamed "The Orphan of the North" because of its isolation. The logging town of Whitney, the largest town in the Upper Madawaska, is located near Airy's northwestern corner. "Airy" conjures up visions of the vast North, but the name actually comes from a highly unlikely source: Sir George Airy was the Astronomer-Royal of Britain from 1835 to 1881, and discovered the eye condition called astigmatism. One suspects the noble Airy's closest encounter with logging was an occasional fox hunt in the New Forest!

AYLEN LAKE. Aylen Lake is a tiny community in Dickens Township, and although the post office recently closed, you can still send letters to Aylen Lake, Ont. The name comes from one of the Ottawa Valley's most notorious figures, lumberjack Peter Aylen. During the 19th century, he was at the centre of the so-called Shiners Wars, a series of bitter confrontations between French and

Irish loggers in the Valley. The conflict was motivated by desperate economic circumstances and racial prejudice, with each group trying to out-muscle the other for logging jobs. Aylen essentially led the Irish faction, and his name was instantly recognized around the Valley for years. Aylen Lake P.O. didn't open until 1955, but the Irishman's name was attached to this lake when he was still known and feared (depending on whether you were Irish or French) in the Upper Madawaska. Another railway station in Renfrew's northernmost township, Clara, was also called Aylen for this lumberman. "Aylen" is usually pronounced with a long "a," "AE-lun."

LYELL. Lyell Township is at the southeastern corner of Nipissing, a short distance from Whitney village. The township is almost uninhabited, and in its 130-odd years has had only one post office, Cross Lake (1900-1918). (As you might expect, Cross Lake is shaped like a cross.) Like some of its immediate neighbors in Hastings, Lyell is named for a famous scientist: Sir Charles Lyell, who lived from 1797 to 1875, was a noted geologist from Scotland. His books *The Principles of Geology* and *The Elements of Geology* were considered the most important geology texts of the early 19th century.

OPEONGO. One of the most famous and recognizable place-names in this region, Opeongo (pronounced "oh-PEE-awng-go") graces two lakes, a river, and a winding settlement road blazed from the Ottawa River into Algonquin Park. The meaning of Opeongo is debatable—G. D. Garland and Alan Rayburn both suggest it is derived from the Ojibwa phrase for "sandy at the narrows." The Opeongo River, Little Opeongo Lake (now called Aylen Lake (see above)) and an old railway station called "Opengo" can be found in the Upper Madawaska. The Opeongo Line still cuts through the Ottawa Valley, starting at the hamlet of Castleford on the Ottawa River and touching communities like Dacre, Clontarf, and Foymount (see Renfrew County for all three). In the 1850s and 1860s, the Line was one of the few links to the outside world for settlers here. Opeongo Lake in Algonquin Park was the first feature to have this place-name, the others being named for their proximity to the lake. The Line was intended to reach Opeongo Lake, but never did.

SABINE. The Township of Sabine is in the southwestern corner of Nipissing District, right next to Hastings County. Sabine has only a few dozen permanent residents, a few of whom lived at Princes Lake. The township takes its name from an English scientist and military officer, Gen. Sir Edward Sabine (1786-1883). Sabine fits into the local pattern of township names here, most of which come from well-known scientists of the 19th century.

The Ones That Got Away

As I wrote this book, a number of place names I wanted to include proved too difficult to track down. Most of these names have been out of use for decades, and there may not be anyone left who remembers them. I've included them in this chapter in hopes someone reading may recognize one of them. If you do have information on any of these names, you should contact the Federal Permanent Committee on Geographic Names, at Room 650, 615 Booth Street, Ottawa, ON K1A 0E9, or the Ontario Geographic Names Board at the Ministry of Natural Resources, 90 Sheppard Avenue East, North York, ON M2N 3A1. They'd love to hear from you.

BALLAVIELLEN. Williamstown, Glengarry County, was briefly known as "Ballaviellen" in 1833. The name looks Irish, but how likely is an Irish name in overwhelmingly Scottish Glengarry? Is this name some relation to Carleton's Ballinvilla?

BANTA. Banta Road in Warkworth, Northumberland County, apparently led to a "Banta hamlet." The hamlet is mentioned in a Centennial year history of Northumberland, but no where else. I do know the road used to be called Banty . . . I'd guess there was a French family named Banté there at one time.

BARB. This curiously named post office was originally known as "East Hawkesbury" from its location in East Hawkesbury Township. The name was changed to Barb by a new postmaster, Michael Maneely, who apparently had five daughters . . . could one of them been <u>Barb</u>ara? Maneely also served in the British army in India, so perhaps there's an Indian connection.

BATTLE HALL. An old postal name from Dalton Township, Victoria County, in use from 1886 to 1891. The hamlet is now known as Ragged Rapids, which became the post office name in 1891. I couldn't find a single piece of information relating to "Battle Hall." Any guesses, folks?

CLABO. Another lost cause from Victoria County. I was told that an intersection near the southern boundary of Ops Township was once called "Clabo." I think the name's Scottish, but there doesn't seem to be any place, building, or person from Scottish history named "Clabo." There wasn't a Clabo Post Office, so no help from that quarter either.

DULCEMAINE. I found the origin of Dulcemaine, thanks to the Front of Leeds & Lansdowne Historical Society. An early settler, walking from Warburton to Lansdowne in Leeds County, said the countryside reminded him of Dulcemaine, Ireland. There's only one problem—there isn't a place called "Dulcemaine" in Ireland! Anyone know of an Irish Dulcemaine?

DVIRNA HILL. This was originally the name of the Perrytown Orange Lodge in Hope Township. The area around the Lodge later became known as "Dvirna Hill" as well. Is there some Orange connection I'm missing here?

FENELLA. This village in Haldimand Township, Northumberland County, seems to have been named for a woman, possibly a female settler in the area. Unfortunately, no one knows who she is today.

FICKO. A hamlet in the city of Gloucester. What the heck's a FICKO?!

GEMLEY. Gemley was the first post office opened in Clarendon & Miller Township. The office was at Playfair Corners, the intersection of the Frontenac and Snow Settlement Roads, in Miller. Gemley only lasted eleven years (1865-1876) and no one today seems to know where the name "Gemley" came from. It would have been much more helpful if it had just been called Playfair Corners!

GLEN ALDA. I want to thank the residents of Chandos Township for their brainstorming about Glen Alda, which so far remains unidentified. The hamlet is on Highway 620 near the Chandos-Wollaston townline, and had a post office until 1950. The first postmaster was a settler named Ira Rosebush. I found a Glen Aldie in Scotland, and a Glen Aulin in the States, but no Glen Alda.

GLOUROURIN. A tongue-twisting school section name from Hamilton Township, Northumberland County. (I feel sorry for the kids who used to have to say it!) I'm convinced this name is Cornish, and there were a large number of Cornish settlers in central Northumberland. But I couldn't find a Glourourin in Cornwall.

HEARTS DESIRE. A very attractive name from Nepean, which unfortunately doesn't seem to have an origin attached to it. There is a place called Hearts Desire in Newfoundland, though it's not clear how or why the name could have ended up here.

IRENA. A Matilda Township post office from 1877 to 1914. Who's Irena? No one seems to remember.

LOST NATION. One of my favorite place-names from Renfrew, Lost Nation is a remote hamlet in central Brudenell Township. Any guesses at to what the "lost nation" is?

PRINCES LAKE. Who are the "Princes" of this lake in the Upper Madawaska?

Sources

Primary Sources.

Files of the Haliburton Highlands Museum, Haliburton, Ont.
Files of the Canadian Permanent Committee on Geographical Names.
Files of the Ontario Geographic Names Board.

Personal correspondence or interviews: Ardoch Algonquin First Nation; D. M. Agnew; Ian Bowering and the Stormont, Dundas & Glengarry Historical Society; S. Brisson; Staff, Township of Chandos; Cliff Couch; Cobourg & District Historical Society; Pauline d'Aoust; Staff, Township of Dummer; Prof. Bruce Elliott; Bill Fitsell; Staff, Township of Front of Leeds & Lansdowne; Hilda Geddes; Greater Harvey Historical Society; Stephen Hill and the staff of the Haliburton Highlands Museum; Kathee Hutcheon; Elizabeth Jones; Fran Laflamme; Gord Martin; Bill McCormick; Mark McMillan; Elizabeth Mitchell; Lois Munro; Marland Murray; the Oso Township Historical Society; E. Pauline Rankin; Alan Rayburn; Jane Rolfe; Viola Seitz; Sgt. Mike Valley; Bill Watt; Allison Willis, Hastings County Museum.

Postmarks provided courtesy the postmasters of: Apple Hill, Ardoch, Astra, Bolsover, Buckhorn, Carp, Carrying Place, Cavan, Chute à Blondeau, Cloyne, Coboconk, Consecon, Corbyville, Cormac, Denbigh, Deux-Rivières, Douro, Dunvegan, Eldorado, Embrun, Enterprise, Gooderham, Inkerman, Irondale, Kinmount, L'Amable, L'Orignal, Lyndhurst, Maynooth, Monkland, Mountain, Pontypool, Quadeville, St-Isidore, St-Paschal-Baylon, Sarsfield, Stonecliffe, Tichborne, Vernon, Wilberforce, Wilno, and Yarker. Postmarks also courtesy Dan McInnis, Sudbury; and Don McPhee, Belleville.

Secondary Sources.

Along the Madawaska: A History of the Townships of Griffith & Matawatchan. Sharbot Lake: Corporation of the Townships of Griffith & Matawatchan, 1983.

Argyris, Eileen. *Cramahe Township.* (Self-Published, originally a series of columns in the Colborne Chronicle.) 1992.

Armstrong, C. A. *Away Back in Clarendon & Miller.* Sharbot Lake: North Frontenac Printing Service, 1976.

Baker, R. H. *A Brief History of Names in the County of Haliburton, With the Dates of First Improvements in County and Townships.* Minden: Minden Echo, 1931 (?).

Beach, Russel, ed. *Touring Guide to Ireland.* Basingstoke, U.K.: The Automobile Association, 1976.

Borg, Ronald, ed. *Peterborough: Land of Shining Waters.* Peterborough: The City and County of Peterborough, 1967.

Boyce, Gerald. *Historic Hastings.* Belleville: Hastings County Council, 1967.

Brault, Lucien. *Histoire des Comtés Unis de Prescott et de Russell*. L'Orignal: Prescott & Russell County Council, 1965.

Broughton, Scotty, ed. *The History of Cramahe Township: 1792-1988*. Cobourg: Township of Cramahe, 1988.

Brown, Gene, and Nadine Brumell, eds. *The Oxen & The Axe*. Madoc: Madoc Review, Ltd., 1965.

Brown, Ron. *Ghost Towns of Ontario*, Vols. 1 & 2. Toronto: Cannonbooks, 1978 and 1983.

Brown, Quentin, ed. *This Green & Pleasant Land: Chronicles of Cavan*. Millbrook, Ont.: Millbrook and Cavan Historical Society, 1990.

Bukle, Ethel. *In and Around Canton*. (Self-Published.) 1989.

Camden Township History Committee. *Camden Township History*. Centreville: The Grindstone, 1970.

Canada. Dept. of Energy, Mines & Resources. *Gazetteer of Canada: Ontario*. Ottawa: Ministry of Supply & Services, 1988.

Canniff, William. *The Settlement of Upper Canada*. Toronto: 1869. Reprinted by Mika, Belleville, 1972.

Carr, Evie. *Ops: Land of Plenty*. Ops Township Council, 1968.

Carr, Violet. *The Rolling Hills*. Manvers Township Council, 1967.

Carter, Floreen. *Ghost and Post Offices of Ontario*. Burlington: Personal Impressions Printing, 1986.

Carter, Floreen. *Place Names of Ontario*. Burlington: Phelps Publishing Co., 1984.

Cole, Jean Murray. *Origins: The History of Dummer Township*. Township of Dummer, 1993.

Croil, James. *Dundas: or, A Sketch of Canadian History*. Montréal: B. Dawson & Son, 1861. Reprinted by Mika, Belleville, 1972.

Cummings, H. R. *Early Days in Haliburton*. Ontario: Department of Lands and Forests, 1962.

Davies, David W. *The World of the Elzevirs*. The Hague: Martinus Nijhoff Press, 1954.

Diack, Francis. *The Inscriptions of Pictland*. Aberdeen: The Third Spalding Book Club, 1944.

Dod, Charles. *The Peerage, Baronetage and Knightage of Great Britain and Ireland*. London: Whittaker & Co., 1854.

Douglas, Sue. *Memories of Somerville Township*. Somerville Township Bicentennial Committee, 1984.

Earle, Evelyn Purvis. *Leeds the Lovely*. 2nd ed. Prescott: St. Lawrence Printing Co., 1974.

Edwards, Frank B. *The Smiling Wilderness: An Illustrated History of Lennox & Addington County*. Camden East: Camden House Publishing, 1984.

Ekwall, Eilert. *Concise Oxford Dictionary of English Place-Names*. Oxford: Clarendon Press, 1951.

Ekwall, Eilert. *English River Names*. Oxford, U.K.: Clarendon Press, 1928. Reprinted 1968.

Elliott, Bruce S. *The City Beyond: A History of Nepean*. Nepean: City of Nepean, 1991.

Emond, Doris M. *I Wonder What Happened to Philip*. (Self-Published.) 1985.

Faulkner, Blanche, and Rosella Clancy. *The Heritage Years: A History of Stirling and District*. Stirling: Stirling Historical Book Committee, 1984.

Field, John. *Place Names of Great Britain and Ireland*. Newton Abbot, U.K.: David & Charles, 1980.

Fleming, Laurel. *Hearth & Heritage: A History of Chaffey's Lock and Area, 1800-1980*. Kingston: Brown & Martin, 1981.

Fleming, Rae. *Eldon Connections*. (Self-Published.) n.d.

Gardiner, Herbert F. *Nothing But Names*. Toronto: George N. Morang & Co., Ltd., 1899.

Garland, G. D. *Names of Algonquin*. Ontario Ministry of Natural Resources, 1991.

Geddes, Hilda. *The Canadian Mississippi River*. Burnstown: General Store Publishing, 1992.

Gibbs, Vicary, and H. A. Doubleday, eds. *The Complete Peerage*. London: St. Catherine Press, 1921.

Harkness, John Graham. *Stormont, Dundas & Glengarry: A History, 1784-1945*. Ottawa: Mutual Press, 1946.

Herrington, Walter S. *History of the County of Lennox & Addington*. Toronto: McMillan, 1913. Reprinted by Mika, Belleville, 1972.

Historic Prince Edward. Prince Edward County Historical Society, 1976.

Historical Glimpses of Lennox & Addington County. Napanee: Lennox & Addington County Council, 1967.

The Illustrated Atlas of Lanark County. Toronto: H. Belden & Co., 1881.

The Illustrated Historical Atlas of the County of Carleton. Toronto: H. Belden & Co., 1879. Reprinted by Mika, Belleville, 1971.

Illustrated Historical Atlas of the Counties of Frontenac and Lennox & Addington. Toronto: H. Beldon & Co., 1878.

Illustrated Historical Atlas of the Counties of Hastings and Prince Edward. Toronto: H. Beldon & Co., 1878.

Illustrated Historical Atlas of the Counties of Leeds & Grenville. Kingston: Putnam & Walling, 1861-62. Reprinted by Mika, Belleville, 1973.

Illustrated Historical Atlas of the Counties of Northumberland and Durham. Toronto: H. Beldon & Co., 1878. Reprinted by Mika, 1972.

Irwin, Ross W. *Mariposa: The Banner Township*. Lindsay: Self-Published, 1984.

Joyce, Patrick Weston. *Pocket Guide to Irish Place Names*. Originally published as *Irish Local Names Explained* (1870). Belfast: Appletree Press, 1984.

Kane, Joseph. *The American Counties*. 3rd ed. Metuchen, NJ: Scarecrow Press, 1972.

Kennedy, Clyde C. *The Upper Ottawa Valley*. Pembroke, ON: Renfrew County Council, 1970.

Kirkconnell, Watson, and F. L. MacArthur. *County of Victoria Centennial History*. Lindsay: Victoria County Council, 1947.

Lapierre, André. *Toponymie française en Ontario*. Montréal: Editions Études vivantes, 1981.

Leavitt, Thad. *History of Leeds & Grenville*. Originally published 1879, reprinted by Mika, Belleville, 1972.

Lee, Sir Sidney. *The Dictionary of National Biography*. 2nd ed. London: Oxford University Press, 1969.

Lee-Whiting, Brenda. *Harvest of Stones*. Toronto: University of Toronto Press, 1985.

Legget, Robert. *Rideau Waterway*. Rev. ed. Toronto: University of Toronto Press, 1972.

Lockwood, Glenn J. "The Pattern of Settlement in Eastern Ontario 1784-1875." *Families*. Vol. 30, No. 4 (November 1991): 235-57.

Lockwood, Glenn J. *Beckwith: Irish and Scottish Identities in a Canadian Community 1816-1991*. Carleton Place: Township of Beckwith, 1991.

Mason, Oliver, ed. *Bartholemew Gazetteer of Britain*. Edinburgh: John Bartholemew & Son, 1977.

McCuaig, D. W., and Carol Bennett. *In Search of Lanark*. Renfrew: Juniper Books, 1982.

McCuaig, D. W., and Carol Bennett. *In Search of the K&P*. Renfrew: Juniper Books, 1982.

McCuaig, D. W., and Carol Bennett. *Renfrew County People & Places*. Renfrew: Juniper Books, 1989.

McKenzie, Ruth. *Leeds & Grenville: Their First 200 Years*. Toronto: McClelland & Stewart, 1967.

Metcalfe, Willis. *Canvas & Steam on Quinte Waters II*. Picton: The Prince Edward Historical Society, 1968.

Mika, Nick, and Helma Mika. *Community Spotlight*. Belleville: Mika, 1974.

Mika, Nick, and Helma Mika. *Places In Ontario, Vols. 1-3*. Belleville: Mika, 1977-1983.

Mika, Nick, and Helma Mika. *Prince Edward County Heritage*. Belleville: Mika, 1980.

Miller, Scott. *An Analysis of Place Names in Carleton County*. Unpublished paper, Carleton University, March, 1973.

Mills, A. D. *Dictionary of English Place Names*. London: Oxford University Press, 1991.

Milne, Catherine. *Village Settlements of Hamilton Township*. Bewdley, Ont.: Clay Publishing, 1991.

Montgomery, Aileen. *The History of Lake Eloida*. Athens: The Athens Reporter, 1961.

Ordnance Survey Gazetteer of Great Britain. 1987.

Oborne, J. Ross. "Festubert: A Wistful Memory of an Earlier Time." *The Canadian Philatelist*. Vol. 42, No. 3 (May-June 1991): 220-2.

Patterson, Neil, ed. *History of the Township of Kingston*. Kingston: Corporation of the Township of Kingston, 1985.

Perly's Detail Atlas of the Province of Ontario. Toronto: Perly's Variprint, n.d.

Poole, Thomas W. *The Early Settlement of Peterborough County*. Peterborough: 1867. Reprinted by the Peterborough Printing Company, 1967.

Rayburn, Alan. *Geographical Names of Renfrew County*. Ottawa: Department of Energy, Mines & Resources, 1967.

Rayburn, Alan. *Lost Names and Places of Eastern Ontario*. Toronto: Ontario Genealogical Society, 1993.

Reeve, Harold. *A History of the Township of Hope*. Cobourg: Cobourg Sentinel-Star, 1967.

Reynolds, Nila. *In Quest of Yesterday.* Lindsay: Provisional County of Haliburton, 1973.

Robinson, Percy J. "Montréal to Niagara in the Seventeenth Century: A Philological Excursion." *Proceedings & Transactions of the Royal Society of Canada.* Vol. 37 (1944): 137-154.

Rollason, Bryan, ed. *County of a Thousand Lakes: The History of the County of Frontenac, 1673-1973.* Kingston: Frontenac County Council, 1982.

Room, Adrian. *A Dictionary of Place Names in the British Isles.* London: Bloomsbury, 1988.

Rosenthal, Max. "The First Post Offices In Lennox & Addington County." *Canadian Philatelist.* Vol. 26 #2 (1975): 83, 85; Vol. 26 #4 (1975): 236-7; Vol. 27 #1 (1976): 48-9; Vol. 27 #2 (1976): 124.

Ross, Ewan. *Glengarry Place Names.* Unpublished Paper, SDG Historical Society.

Schmid, Helen, and Sid Rutherford. *Out of the Mists: A History of Clarke Township.* Orono: Orono Weekly Times, 1976.

Seltzer, Leon, ed. *The Columbia Lippincott Gazetteer of the World.* Morningside Heights, NY: Columbia University Press, 1962.

Sills, Luella, and Margaret Smith. *Foxboro: Portrait of a Village.* Foxboro: Emmanuel United Church, 1975.

Smith, Robert. *Ontario Post Offices.* Vol. ii. Toronto: The Unitrade Press, 1988.

Smith, Susan W. *The First Summer People.* Toronto: Boston Mills Press, 1993.

Stewart, George R. *American Place-Names.* New York: Oxford University Press, 1970.

Suggitt, Gladys M. *Roses and Thorns: A Goodly Heritage.* Peterborough: Color Reproductions, Ltd., 1972.

Sylvester, Thomas Wm. *Amherst Island: A Detailed Survey [Sir John Johnson] circa 1790 and Land Ownership.* Stella: Curbside Publishing, 1993.

Ten Cate, Adrian, ed. *A Pictorial History of the Thousands Islands of the St. Lawrence River.* Brockville: Besancourt Publishers, 1977.

Theberge, Clifford, and Elaine Theberge. *The Trent-Severn Waterway: A Traveller's Companion.* Toronto: Samuel-Stevens, Publishers, 1978.

"There's this story about a dog..." *Haliburton County Echo,* September 11, 1990.

Turner, Larry. *Ernestown: Rural Spaces, Urban Places.* Toronto: Dundurn Press, 1993.

Two Centuries of Change: United Counties of Northumberland and Durham, 1767-1967. Cobourg: United Counties Centennial Book Committee, 1967.

Waldman, Carl. *Word Dance: The Language of Native American Culture.* New York: Facts on File, 1994.

Wilkins, Taylor. *Haliburton by Rail and the I.B.&O.* Lindsay: John Deyell Co., 1992.

Zandbergen, Lewis. "A short history of Foxboro." *The Community Press,* 16 September 1986.

Index

About the Author

Michael Dawber is a freelance journalist and editor specializing in the local history and place names of Eastern Ontario. Born in Kingston in 1970, Dawber grew up in Bakers Hill, a small rural hamlet just west of that city. Since graduating from Carleton University's School of Journalism in 1993, he has written three books and numerous articles on the history of the province. His published works include two travel guides and a biography of Mrs. Rae Luckock, Ontario's first female legislator. Dawber has taken a particular interest in the old Kick & Push Railway line, which once ran from Kingston to Renfrew, and he now lives near the Kick & Push in Snow Road Station, Ontario

To order more copies of

Where the Heck is
BALAHECK?

send $14.95 plus $3.00 to cover
GST, shipping and handling to:

General Store Publishing House
1 Main Street, Burnstown, Ontario
K0J 1G0

Telephone: 1-800-465-6072
Fax: 613-432-7184